Yeats's Early Poetry

YEATS'S EARLY POETRY

The Quest for Reconciliation

FRANK HUGHES MURPHY

Louisiana State University Press

BATON ROUGE

ISBN 0–8071–0091–9
Library of Congress Catalog Card Number 73–90864
Copyright © 1975 by Louisiana State University Press
All rights reserved
Manufactured in the United States of America

This book was designed by Dwight Agner. It was set in
Linotype Times Roman with Deepdene display and
printed on Warren Olde Style paper by Moran Industries, Inc.,
Baton Rouge, Louisiana.

This book is for

JAMES EDWARD McSWEENEY

Contents

	Acknowledgments	ix
	Introduction	1
1	The Earliest Poetry: CROSSWAYS	7
2	THE ROSE and the Quest for Eternal Beauty	31
3	THE WIND AMONG THE REEDS and Apocalyptic Vision	65
4	A New Voice for the Old Bitterness, 1904–1910	87
5	RESPONSIBILITIES: The Poet as Visionary Reformer	115
6	The Early *Vision* Poems: Culmination of the Quest	137
	Index	169

Acknowledgments

I AM ESPECIALLY grateful to Professor Richard Harter Fogle of the University of North Carolina for his perceptive and kindly guidance during the preparation of an earlier version of this study; to my friend and colleague David M. Bergeron of the University of New Orleans for his multiple role as stylistic advisor, proofreader, and patient listener; and to my wife Catherine for generous and loving support during every phase of my work.

Grateful acknowledgment is offered to the Macmillan Company for permission to reprint quotations from the following works by William Butler Yeats:

The Autobiography of William Butler Yeats. Copyright 1916, 1935 by the Macmillan Company; copyright 1924 by the Dial Publishing Company; copyright renewed 1944, 1952, 1963 by Bertha Georgie Yeats; copyright © 1965 by the Macmillan Company.

A Vision. Copyright 1937 by the Macmillan Company; copyright 1938 by William Butler Yeats; copyright renewed 1965 by Bertha Georgie Yeats and Anne Butler Yeats.

Acknowledgments

The Collected Poems of W. B. Yeats. Copyright 1903, 1906, 1907, 1912, 1916, 1918, 1919, 1924, 1928, 1931, 1933, 1934, 1935, 1940, 1944, 1945, 1946, 1950, 1956 by the Macmillan Company; copyright 1940 by Georgie Yeats; definitive edition, with the author's final revisions, copyright © 1956 by the Macmillan Company.

Essays and Introductions. Copyright © 1961 by Mrs. W. B. Yeats.

The Letters of W. B. Yeats, edited by Allan Wade. Copyright 1953, 1954 by Anne Butler Yeats.

The Variorum Edition of the Poems of W. B. Yeats, edited by Peter Allt and Russell K. Alspach. Copyright 1903, 1906, 1907, 1912, 1916, 1918, 1919, 1924, 1928, 1931, 1933, 1934, 1935, 1940, 1944, 1945, 1946, 1950, 1956, 1957 by the Macmillan Company; copyright 1940 by Georgie Yeats.

Yeats's Early Poetry

Introduction

FROM THE PUBLICATION of his first poems in 1885 to his death in 1939, Yeats's long poetic career reflects his effort to discover an imaginative means of reconciling apparent antinomies. Indeed, perhaps the most characteristic single element in his poetry is his preoccupation with the dualistic nature of experience. Among the most recurrent of the antinomial pairs which concerned him were the ideal and the real, escape and involvement, imagination and intellect, and contemplation and action—many of them apparently so closely related in Yeats's mind as to become synonymous. His poems frequently reveal such fusions as the imaginative with the ideal, or the intellectual with the real. Yeats makes his recognition of these relationships explicit in *A Vision*, grouping the forces in two opposing camps which he labels the primary and the antithetical.

At various times Yeats pronounces himself an advocate of one side or the other; and it is not surprising that he, being a poet in the Romantic tradition, is personally committed to the side of imagination and ideal beauty, for example, rather than to that of rational intellect and the ugliness of the actual. But his pro-

1

nouncements of preference are mostly restricted to his personal life; in the poems themselves the antinomies are too fundamental, too crucial a problem to be judged and dismissed through such an easy resolution as private preference. Rather, the antinomies continue to defy either a resolution in which one side can be chosen and the other safely rejected, or a dissolution into some expansive unity that can encompass both. Even in *A Vision*, where Yeats scrupulously grants equal importance to the primary and the antithetical, it is clear that he, being himself an antithetical personality, loads the options in favor of the latter.

The poetry, then, becomes the perpetual battleground upon which opposing forces meet—body against soul, reason against dream, selflessness against ego. Whenever a single poem suggests a victory, another poem fast behind it renews the conflict. This sense of duality seems profoundly disturbing to Yeats, for it represents to him a division, a fragmentation of human experience, whereas his imagination, fed upon Blake and Shelley, dictates the need for unity and perfection. Everywhere in his early poetry one finds evidence of this restless dissatisfaction with a world of battling contraries. The earliest effort to come to terms with these contraries is an experimental investigation of pure aestheticism, for which many critics have harshly condemned Yeats as an "escapist," despite the fact (as I see it) that escapism never satisfies him. The land of perpetual dancing beyond the sea (as in THE WANDERINGS OF OISIN), like Yeats's other variants of the Irish never-never land of Tir-na'n Og, must finally fail to satisfy the visitor from the shattered world of creation, and that visitor must ultimately return whence he came. After this period of experimentation, Yeats confronts the world of experience through passionate involvement in political and cultural activity which is meant to save his fellow men from their destructive bent. There are also more personal attempts at reconciliation, such as his determined faith in immortality as a defense against mutability and death. And through most of his life Yeats seeks a spiritual revelation that will at last enable him to perceive a means of universal reconciliation.

His quest for reconciliation leads him down many strange paths, among them his membership in such hermetic societies as the Rosicrucian Order of the Golden Dawn and Madame Blavatsky's Theosophical Society. The quest culminates in perhaps the strangest path of all: his wife's supernaturally inspired dictation of the material that became *A Vision*—that troublesome book which, as Yeats himself puts it, reflects his effort "to hold in a single thought reality and justice."[1] The completed *Vision*, that is, will lead him to reconcile through his imagination the harshness of reality with a notion of justice that is not readily observable in that reality.

As Yeats grows more and more deeply absorbed in the *Vision* material, his own vision broadens into a perplexed recognition of universal conflict and mutability as the necessary design of the universe. The comprehensive and rigid philosophical system of *A Vision* leads him, finally, to embrace both what he loves and what he despises. The ever-widening implications of this system demonstrate his remarkable development from a utopian dreamer (though one for whom dream alone is never enough) to a kind of prophet who ultimately rejects nothing and would balance all contraries. The final revelation of the system, however, instead of offering a Romantic reunification of the fragmented universe, offers only an insight into the inescapable fact of universal conflict and mutability: fragments that never arrive at wholeness, but struggle eternally toward that condition. In reading *A Vision* one may sense, as I do, that Yeats's Thirteenth Cone, which is the final resting place for human souls once they have completed their labyrinthine circuit of successive incarnations, is disappoint-

---

1 W. B. Yeats, *A Vision* (Rev. ed.; New York: Macmillan, 1937), 25.

ingly static and may represent the seed of Yeats's own disenchant-
ment with the system as an explanation of human destiny. At any
rate, even though the original and revised versions of this book
absorbed Yeats's imagination and energy for twenty years, *A Vision* seems to be for him a source of "metaphors for poetry" (as
he describes its usefulness) rather than a final view of cosmology.

The purpose of this study is to trace Yeats's efforts toward an
ultimate reconciliation of the contrary forces of human experience
as they are reflected in the first eight groups of his lyric poetry as
arranged in *The Collected Poems*—from the earliest CROSSWAYS
through MICHAEL ROBARTES AND THE DANCER.[2] Although there
are now several excellent studies of Yeats's early poetry, there
remains a disturbing tendency among scholars to dismiss the
early poetry under such labels as escapist, imitative, immature.
Instead of viewing these poems merely as precursors of the later,
more famous poetry, and instead of exploring them for evidence
of biographical and literary influences upon Yeats's style, I have
confined myself for the most part to close readings of the individual poems, because I am convinced of their ability to sustain close
analysis with little more than passing reference to the later work.

The various private means of reconciliation that Yeats proposes
and then partially rejects, the various poetic approaches he adopts
in an effort to achieve some imaginative resolution—all reveal
a mind that is not merely restless (though it is certainly that),
but one possessed of a driving energy that can tolerate anything
but stasis, anything but complacency. His progress—as we shall
see in the individual poems and in the larger patterns embodied
in them—moves always toward greater inclusiveness, despite

---

2 Variant versions of a poem will generally be ignored in favor of the
final versions in *The Collected Poems* (New York: Macmillan, 1956),
unless the original was significantly different in meaning or in form
and unless the difference is relevant to my discussion. Where variant
versions are cited, they are taken from Peter Allt and Russell K.
Alspach (eds.), *The Variorum Edition of the Poems of W. B. Yeats*
(New York: Macmillan, 1968).

traumatic setbacks such as that recorded in THE WIND AMONG THE REEDS. Thus, at the climax of his quest, in *A Vision*, he is able for the moment to reject nothing that is part of the human experience —to embrace all of hate, all of love, the actual and the ideal, in one consummate vision.

1

The Earliest Poetry:
CROSSWAYS

EXCEPT for THE WANDERINGS OF OISIN, Yeats includes all of those poems written in the 1880s that he considers worthy to survive in the CROSSWAYS section of the definitive edition of his poetry. Most of these sixteen early works deserve careful attention, not only because they are good poems frequently slighted by commentators, but also because they reveal that a surprising number of Yeats's mature ideas about life and poetry had already been formulated early in his career. In view of the unusual length of his poetic career, characterized by abrupt shifts in style, symbolism, and ideology, it is easy to overlook the fact that his early work shares so much with his later work. Richard Ellmann stresses this point: "Changes in diction are likely to blind us to the constancy of themes. The substitution of one symbol for another is likely to conceal their equivalence."[1] Yeats himself writes to Olivia Shakespear (June 30, 1932), while preparing the definitive edition of his poetry: "I have just finished the first volume, all my lyric poetry, and am greatly astonished at myself. ... I

---

1 Richard Ellmann, *The Identity of Yeats* (New York: Oxford University Press, 1964), 1.

keep saying what man is this who . . . says the same thing in so many different ways."[2]

Underlying the CROSSWAYS poems, and indeed all of Yeats's work, is the assumption that there is some transcendent unity which will embrace the seemingly irreconcilable antinomies of the real and the ideal. Most of the poems discussed in this chapter offer a harsh and dissatisfied appraisal of the human condition; and each poem pushes toward some form of reconciliation of opposites that will restore the balance and unity which exist, so far, only in the poet's own imagination. This search for unity expresses in itself a kind of transcendent reconciliation in these poems; for although ultimate unity may lie far beyond human attainment, it is deemed no less worthy of the poet's commitment, because the poet's imagination insists upon its reality even if it cannot be seen in the limited world of the senses. Ellmann observes that all of Yeats's work "can be read as a concerted effort to bring such contrasting elements as man and divinity, man and woman, man and external nature, man and his ideal, into a single circle."[3]

In the individual poems this search for unity is implied, if not explicit, in Yeats's pursuit of three somewhat less than exalted means of reconciling man to his condition on this earth. These are the comfort of aestheticism, the escape into dream, and the sympathy of nature. In these we find the least aggressive aspect of Yeats's lifelong search for unity and harmony; the poet here seeks sedative rather than cure. But happily, even so young, Yeats is able to perceive the limitations of these three "sedatives" almost as quickly as he considers them. And each of them succumbs to a negative discovery: art, for all its loveliness, proves at best but a fleeting comfort for one who demands total unity; the dream (or the land of dreams) is shattered by the mutability which time imposes—the gradual death of passion, even of love; and nature,

2 Allan Wade (ed.), *The Letters of W. B. Yeats* (New York: Macmillan, 1955), 798.
3 Ellmann, *The Identity of Yeats*, 7.

instead of communicating some form of sympathy for man's loneliness and pain, remains indifferent. Yeats rejects each of these possible sources of reconciliation—not necessarily as without value, but certainly as inadequate to his imaginative need for the restoration of perfect harmony to man and his world.

In this sense Yeats exonerates himself through his earliest works from the frequent accusation that he was an escapist who rejected the world of experience, an aesthete who sought a form of art purged of the imperfections of the everyday occurrences of human life. The most insistent spokesman for this accusation is D. S. Savage, who writes: "Yeats, looking inwards, could see only a static universe of moods and dreams, and this he translated into his work. The repugnance to the world of actuality which aestheticism typifies severely limits the material and scope of art, and in the early Yeats this is restricted to a small range of dream-imagery used to convey a predominant, static emotion of world-weariness and ineffectual and objectless longing."[4]

Certainly the early Yeats is less embroiled in the "world of actuality" than he would be later as a statesman, public orator, champion of nationalist causes, and, as he put it in "Among School Children," "A sixty-year-old smiling public man." This is not surprising in view of the fact that Yeats's earliest poems were written when he was in his early twenties; for world-weariness has been characteristic of young poets throughout history, and especially throughout the 1890s. Shy and self-conscious to an agonizing extreme, Yeats was in the 1880s still an onlooker at this "world of actuality," one who did not particularly admire what he found there. But if his poems of this period do not deal with actual events, they are not for this reason necessarily "escapist" poems. As Louis MacNeice forcefully argues: "We cannot . . . infer . . . that a poem about such an event is necessarily a

4 D. S. Savage, "The Aestheticism of W. B. Yeats," in James Hall and Martin Steinmann (eds.), *The Permanence of Yeats* (New York: Macmillan, 1961), 177.

better poem or a more important or even a more realistic poem than a poem about something far less contemporary or far more obscure or private. . . . I do not think we can say that the poet's reality is . . . less real than the scientist's—unless we are prepared to say that hunger is less real than bread."[5] Yeats's earliest work disproves Savage's suggestion that his was a static universe and a static emotion. Despite the pervasive presence of sighing and dreaming in CROSSWAYS, the careful reader cannot fail to be struck by Yeats's refusal to content himself with a separate peace either through art or dream or escape into nature. The poet holds out with admirable courage for a far more inclusive form of reconciliation, one which will not exclude the ordinary and the dreary, but rather embrace all of human experience into a universal unity. In this sense we see Yeats, even so early, looking forward to the elaborate formulation of the universal system of *A Vision*, which is foreshadowed in many of his first poems.

The striking fact about Yeats's so-called escapist poetry, then, is that in no one poem did mere escapism satisfy him. He considered the possibilities of such a position from every perspective and found it lacking. It is the restless energy of these poems, and not their stasis, which compels our attention. If we mean by escapism that the young Yeats was preoccupied with problems of the spirit rather than with those of the vibrant physical worlds around Dublin and London, then we must find him guilty of the charge; but if we mean, as so many of his accusers do, that he turned away from the real world in favor of a dreamy retreat, a kind of imaginative hibernation, then he rises rather magnificently above the charge from the first CROSSWAYS poem.

The CROSSWAYS poems demonstrate that the reconciliation theme received a highly complex and sophisticated treatment even in the 1880s, a period of his life which even Yeats's most ardent readers often dismiss as a time of idle dreaming. Norman

5 Louis MacNeice, *The Poetry of W. B. Yeats* (New York: Oxford University Press, 1941), 20.

Jeffares represents the majority judgment when he concludes from a reading of "The Song of the Last Arcadian" (to be discussed below under its later title, "The Song of the Happy Shepherd"): "These lines represent Yeats's own attitude to life at the time: words alone are certain good; deeds must not be worshipped, nor truth be hungered after. It was a state of poetic dreaming and escape from life."[6]

Yeats himself was hardly defensive of his early work: "Yet when I re-read those early poems which gave me so much trouble, I find little but romantic convention, unconscious drama."[7] In the first volume of his autobiography he described "The Lake Isle of Innisfree," written in 1890, as "my first lyric with anything in its rhythm of my own music."[8] With such comments he often dismissed the poems of the 1880s as imitative and foreign to his true spirit. My intention is to redeem these early poems from both Yeats's own harsh judgment and Jeffares' representative oversimplification.

The first poem of CROSSWAYS, "The Song of the Happy Shepherd," written in 1885, considers both art and dream as sources for reconciling man to his earthly lot. One of the best known and certainly most complex poems of this early period, "The Song of the Happy Shepherd" has nevertheless been generally ignored by commentators, or dismissed, too hastily, as an easy advocacy of aestheticism and dream.

In the three short sections which comprise the poem, the shepherd (a) laments that the world has turned from dreaming in order to pursue Grey Truth, whereas "Words alone are certain good"; (b) counsels his listener to pursue no truth except that of his own heart and, ignoring men of science, to speak his story into a seashell, which will reword it "in melodious guile"; and

6 Norman Jeffares, *W. B. Yeats: Man and Poet* (2nd ed.; New York: Barnes and Noble, 1966), 30.
7 William Butler Yeats, *The Autobiography of William Butler Yeats* (New York: Macmillan, 1965), 69.
8 *Ibid.*, 103.

finally (c) departs to sing songs of the past over the grave of a faun, reminding his listener to "Dream, dream, for this is also sooth."

It is an oversimplification, first of all, to suppose that the shepherd's song represents Yeats's own attitude. In making this supposition Jeffares does not take into account the poet's frequent use of a persona. In this case Yeats adopts the conventional persona of a naive shepherd (whose counsel is later discredited in a companion poem); elsewhere he speaks through such diverse voices as those of an Indian, the mad King Goll, the Sidhe, an old fisherman, and a peasant woman named Moll Magee. In fact, Yeats is probably more reluctant to speak in his own voice in these early poems than at any other time of his career; hence we must be ever alert for ironies that occur at the expense of the speaker. As Ellmann puts it: "To be successful, the poet must be humble before his own *personae*. In Yeats's verse, we shall find, a series of ideas recur, but they recur as expressions of his characters. . . . The only way in which poetry can be philosophical, Yeats brilliantly declared, is by portraying 'the emotions of a soul dwelling in the presence of certain ideas'." [9]

It is also hazardous to assume too readily that the poem argues against the pursuit of truth. There are two kinds of "truth," one spurious and one valid, identified in the poem; one is the "Grey Truth" which is now the world's toy and which seems to be what the "starry men" seek with their optic glass. Theirs is an undesirable pursuit because it is a fruitless one: ". . . there is no truth / Saving in thine own heart." The men of science have gone astray because "dead is all their human truth." This "human truth" is the second and really the only kind, for Grey Truth is illusory; and human truth can be found only within the self. It is therefore foolish "To hunger fiercely after truth," to explore the outer world for it, because its sources are within. It is not the search

9 Ellmann, *The Identity of Yeats*, 43.

for truth itself that the shepherd condemns, then, but rather a search in the wrong direction.

But how does one gain awareness of this truth which lies within? The shepherd advises, "Dream, dream, for this is also sooth." The poem presents a complex and even confusing treatment of the dream theme, in which dreaming is posed as an alternative to active involvement in the world. Variants of the word *dream* appear nine times in this relatively short lyric, and dream clearly constitutes part of its major theme. On the surface the shepherd's counsel seems clear enough: it is better to dream than to follow the world's vain search after external truth or to worship "dusty deeds." But as so often happens in Yeats's poetry, a closer reading reveals complexities which undercut the surface affirmation. "Of old the world on dreaming fed; / Grey Truth is now her painted toy," the shepherd reflects; "Yet still she turns her restless head." These lines might be paraphrased: "Whereas the world once fed on dreaming, she now toys with truth—but both pastimes have left her restless." The shepherd regrets the shift from dreaming to truth-seeking; but even so, is dreaming—like the pursuit of Grey Truth—only the equivalent of a painted toy? These lines seem to say so.

Savage notes the distinction between *feeding* and *toying*, and he interprets it to mean that dreams are more valuable because they offer real sustenance, not being merely playthings.[10] But why, then, has the world abandoned dream? Why does she still turn her "restless head"? Evidently dreaming was inadequate for her, whatever it may prove to be for this naive young shepherd.

Reinforcing the suggestion that dreaming is an idle pursuit, the shepherd warns against a search after truth: "Lest all thy toiling only breed / New dreams, new dreams." One may as well dream on, for the pursuit of Grey Truth returns him ultimately to dreaming. Such an observation serves not so much to recommend dream

10 Savage, "The Aestheticism of W. B. Yeats," 178.

as to show that scientific truth-seeking is no better than dream. We learn in the final stanza that the shepherd is himself a dreamer, one who dreams that the dead faun still "treads the lawn / Walking ghostly in the dew." Even the songs which he plays for the ghostly faun are "of old earth's dreamy youth." At the end of the poem the shepherd prescribes dreaming for everyone: "Dream thou! / For fair are poppies on the brow: / Dream, dream, for this is also sooth."

But can one be certain that dream leads to subjective truth? The shepherd is not an altogether convincing model of one who gains in truth as he pipes old tunes over a faun's grave, pretending that the faun hears with delight. "Dream" in this case is not a soaring of the imagination, released from the shackles of reason; nor is it even a surrender to fancy, that lower faculty; rather, dreaming is a deliberate deception, a delusory game. The faun is dead, the music is unheard, and the shepherd advances neither in truth nor in wisdom.

Not that Yeats is critical of the idle shepherd, but the poet does remain at a safe aesthetic distance from his persona; he may even envy the shepherd his simplicity and his confidence in dream, but he does not *share* either quality. One further clue to Yeats's intention may lie in the repeated phrase, used almost as a refrain: "For this is also sooth." Since the poem considers a search for truth, the reader may assume that *sooth* bears its usual meaning, *truth*. If, however, one considers the word's second meaning (*soft, sweet*), a teasing ambiguity results: "Dreaming, too, is sweet, is soothing"—even if not truth. If Yeats were conscious of this double meaning (and it is likely that he was, since he delighted in and frequently exploited multiple meanings), we might fairly conclude that the poem ends, not in recommending dream as superior to the pursuit of Grey Truth, but in lowering the scientific quest to the level of dream: both are soothing for a time, but neither is any closer to the final truth and harmony to which the poet's imagination commits him. Dreaming may be as close as we can come toward an image of harmony; but that, like the scientist's goal, may not be very close at all.

Closely allied is a second alternative in the quest for reconciliation in "The Song of the Happy Shepherd": "Words alone are certain good." One of the most frequently quoted lines from any of the CROSSWAYS poems, this generally (and, I believe, wrongly) serves as evidence of Yeats's early aestheticism, a glorification of art for art's sake which he offers with his back turned firmly against the world of men—what Savage refers to as "Yeats's completely impervious aestheticism."[11] MacNeice reports that Sturge Moore quoted this line to him as proof that Yeats belonged to the company of mystics, and MacNeice himself seems to have taken the line as Yeats's own judgment though he concedes that while words remained certain good for Yeats all his life, they were not necessarily alone in being so.[12] Charles Berryman is practically alone in his defense of the line: "Jeffares mistakenly identifies the remark . . . as the full sentiment of the young poet. The biographical critic ignores the poetic context of the shepherd's line. Yeats presents the happy shepherd as a dramatically conceived persona in direct contrast to the character of the sad shepherd. . . . Even Yeats's best critics are prone to identity him merely with the happy shepherd and thus attribute to him the very attitude that Yeats is trying to limit if not repudiate."[13] Did the poet actually propose words alone as a "certain good," a means of reconciliation between imagination and reality? Or can we accept this affirmation any more confidently than the advice to dream?

To answer such questions we must first determine what *good* means in the poem. This is easily done, since we learn that the warring kings of history ("word be-mockers") are gone and that

11 *Ibid.*, 177.
12 MacNeice, *The Poetry of W. B. Yeats*, 31.
13 Charles Berryman, *W. B. Yeats: Design of Opposites* (New York: Exposition Press, 1967), 123.

only "An idle word is now their glory / By the stammering school-boy said." One requisite of the "good" of the poem is apparently permanence, and one problem of the stanza in question is what constitutes immortality. As in Shelley's "Ozymandias," from which Yeats may well have gained inspiration for this part of the poem, the kings of history live on only in words. But are words alone "certain good"? As Yeats pushes the question to larger dimensions, words appear to bear no guarantee of permanence:

> The wandering earth herself may be
> Only a sudden flaming word,
> In clanging space a moment heard,
> Troubling the endless reverie.

In relative terms, the earth may last no longer than the kings did, and the poet's search for some ultimate meaning through a discovery of permanence in observable creation remains unfulfilled.

"Seek, then, for this is also sooth / No word of theirs," we are warned of the scientists; if any word is the good we seek, it is assuredly not theirs, for—as we saw earlier—theirs lacks human truth. "Good" must not only be permanent; it must concern the human spirit. What word, then, is good? The seashell into which the shepherd advises his listener to whisper his tale (an obvious symbol for the transformation of reality achieved through art) scarcely meets the requirement of permanence even if it may abound in human truth. For the shell will repeat the words, melodiously transformed, "a little while / Till they shall singing fade in ruth / And die a pearly brotherhood." No "stammering schoolboy," yet unborn, is likely to chant such an ephemeral tale as this.

The line just quoted—"And die a pearly brotherhood"—is Yeats's substitution for the original line, "For ruth and joy have brotherhood." The original shows how conscious the poet was, even so early in his career, of the curious kinship of opposites and of his need to reconcile them in his poetry. Perhaps the line was deleted because at the time he revised the poem Yeats was struggling to rid himself of abstractions; but whatever the reason, we are left with the curious phrase "pearly brotherhood," which is unlike most of Yeats's revisions in that it is less clear than its predecessor. Yeats was at this time fond of the word *pearly*, one might assume from its recurrence elsewhere in CROSSWAYS; but what it meant to him is unclear. Perhaps the surest and simplest guess is that the mother-of-pearl coloration of the inner surface of certain seashells was on his mind; beyond this, perhaps there was the association of pearl (product of the oyster shell) with art (the echoed tale, product of the seashell). Since it is an "echo-harbouring shell" that the shepherd speaks of, perhaps the "pearly brotherhood" represents all of verbal art—those lingering echoes of other tellers of tales, harbored within the shell, which welcome the newly whispered tale, then die with it. If this rather convoluted reading is at all accurate, then art— which feebly revives and swiftly dies again with each new addition, being perpetually lost rather than perpetually renewed— comes out of the poem as a very dim consolation indeed.

Neither art nor dream, then, satisfies the requisites of the "good" of which the shepherd speaks. Neither is able to achieve the reconciliation which the poet seeks. All this talk of dreaming and of words being "certain good," then, should not distract us from the fact that Yeats himself endorses neither course. Edmund Wilson, in a related discussion, recognizes that Yeats's dreamers are made to tread upon perilous ground:

But just as Yeats's early poetry represents the fascination of fairy-land as something inimical to life in the real world, so these stories of ecstatic revery, unlike the typical writings of the *fin de siècle* aesthetes, are edged with a consciousness of dangers and temptations inescapably involved in such a life. . . . What *is* the consequence of living for beauty . . . as a supreme end in itself? We shall be thrown fatally out of key with reality . . . and Yeats, even in his earliest period, is unceasingly aware of this conflict. [*Then Wilson adds, with some regret:*] But still he prefers to dwell most of the time in fairy-land or among the dancers of the Alchemical Temple.[14]

When Yeats revised the poem sometime between its original publication in the *Dublin University Review* in October, 1885, and its second appearance in *The Wanderings of Oisin and Other Poems* in 1889, he made the poem's attitude toward dream and art more starkly emphatic by omitting the clutter of inessential words and images. None of his fairly extensive revisions significantly change the poem's meaning. The most important changes were the incorporation of simpler diction, a more natural syntax, and a tighter formal structure, one devoid of mere decoration. For example, *pierc'd* becomes the more natural *pierced, 'mong the dew* becomes *in the dew*, the archaic and pseudopoetic *I-wis* is eliminated altogether, and the clumsy inversion *till rise the dawn* becomes simply *before the dawn*. Three lines which referred idly to bees, birds, and a glade disappear from the poem. This avoidance of decoration distinguishes Yeats from those *fin de siècle* aesthetes with whom Savage groups him, whose goals were (according to Savage) "dream and decoration." In choosing this complex and elaborately structured poem to open his collected works, Yeats must surely have meant to demonstrate his early dissatisfaction with languorous aestheticism.

The companion poem to "The Song of the Happy Shepherd" is the second CROSSWAYS poem, "The Sad Shepherd." There are several such pairs of companion poems in this section, the first of each pair bearing approximately the same relation to the second that Blake's *Songs of Innocence* bears to his *Songs of Experience*.[15] This arrangement suggests that Yeats was deliberately posing opposite forces against each other, and that his final

14 Edmund Wilson, "W. B. Yeats," in Hall and Steinmann (eds.), *The Permanence of Yeats*, 19.

15 Harold Bloom would disagree with this suggestion, having sensed parallels between CROSSWAYS and *Songs of Innocence*, and THE ROSE and *Songs of Experience*. His position is expressed in his book *Yeats* (New York: Oxford University Press, 1970), 105.

thematic intention for any one of these poems cannot be determined without considering its companion—any more than Blake's can be determined without the same consideration. To make the analogy more explicit, one might say that it would be as unwise to view "The Happy Shepherd" without considering "The Sad Shepherd" as it would be to view "The Lamb" without "The Tyger."

"The Sad Shepherd" presents an altogether different view of the circumstance expressed in the previous poem. This second poem reveals the sad disparity between song and reality: whereas the first shepherd advised his listener to dream and to speak his sad tale into a seashell, the second shepherd—in taking the advice—gains no comfort at all. While the happy shepherd is lost in dream, the sad shepherd is his opposite—in later years Yeats would have called him the happy shepherd's mask—who is so sunken into the world of experience that there is no opportunity for escape even through dream. He bears his sorrow first to the stars, then the sea, the dewdrops, and finally the seashell—but he encounters only universal indifference. There is not even the brief comfort that had been promised him ("And they thy comforters will be, / . . . Till they shall singing fade in ruth."). Instead of transforming his words "in melodious guile," the shell—with its "hollow pearly heart"—turns all to "inarticulate moan." John Unterecker, one of the few who have commented on the kinship of the two poems, suggests that the sad shepherd fails because he is not an artist, and that this is what separates him from his happier counterpart in the other poem.[16] I find no specific evidence to support this view, though the continuing contrasts between dream and reality, as represented by other pairs of CROSSWAYS poems, do suggest that the first shepherd represents the dreamer and the second, the disillusioned realist who is eager to dream but is denied its limited consolation.

16 John Unterecker, *A Reader's Guide to William Butler Yeats* (New York: Noonday Press, 1959), 68.

Art as a means of reconciliation gains no further attention in the CROSSWAYS poems, but escapism of a kind appears in many other poems, often involving a misty paradise which can only be interpreted as a dreamland or fairyland (variations upon the Irish mythological Tir-na'n Og). The element of withdrawal appears even in many poems which do not deal directly with an escape into dream or fairyland, and this element lends a peculiar withdrawn quality to almost all of the CROSSWAYS poems. One key image which signals this withdrawal is the strangely persistent setting of a shoreline or border. None of the characters in these poems lives in the midst of turbulent humanity; rather, all exist along the fringes of the busy world.

In "Anashuya and Vijaya," for example, one member of the lovers' triangle lives on the border of the village and another lives in the forest—a distinction which may suggest their relative degrees of involvement with the world of men. Typical of Yeats's lovers, neither of the women lives in the midst of village life. In "The Indian upon God," the speaker overhears the various animals and plants speculating about the nature of divinity as he passes "along the water's edge," again suggesting a separation from normal human activity, one which has probably led him into such a peculiar experience in the first place. In "The Indian to His Love," the two lovers walk together "by the water's drowsy blaze"; and in "Ephemera," these (presumably) same two lovers stand "by the lone border of the lake." In both the passion of young love and the disillusionment that follows, they are set apart from the rest of the world. The Sidhe in "The Stolen Child" conceal their "faery vats," we are told, on the shore of a leafy island—suggesting, perhaps, the mystic enchantment in store for those who stray from the tumult of life. "To an Isle in the Water" reveals its setting in its title. In "Down by the Salley Gardens," the lovers have stood in happier days "in a field by the river," just as in "The Meditation of the Old Fisherman" the old man recalls past lovers "Who paced in the eve by the nets on the pebbly shore." There is no advantage in attempting to define this persistent image as a specific symbol, for it seems more suggestive than precise. But what it suggests—the isolation of almost all of Yeats's early characters—is well worth noting, for it indicates a fragmentation of experience and a need for some form of reconciliation between these isolated characters and normal human society.

It is not simply that the characters live in isolation, however; frequently they have been driven into it by shattering experiences within society. Almost all of the CROSSWAYS characters have been displaced in some way from active roles in life. A mad old king ("The Madness of King Goll") has abandoned his kingship to roam the wilds. A forlorn peasant woman ("The Ballad of Moll Magee") has accidentally killed her infant daughter and, in exile from her wrathful husband, wanders the countryside seeking comfort. Naive lovers smugly congratulate themselves on their isolation from the "unquiet lands" ("The Indian to His Love"), only to wither later within that same isolation ("Ephemera"). An old fisherman ("The Meditation of the Old Fisherman") senses his displacement from the intensity of his youth as he endures the pallid present time. The forlorn, lonely shepherd and the happy one who pipes for the dead faun are both isolated in a conventional pastoral setting. A priest ("The Ballad of Father O'Hart") has been cast away from and denied the use of his own land. Almost the only exception is the foxhunter ("The Ballad of the Foxhunter"), who dies contented after a full and active life. But this poem, like the preceding one, was an addition to CROSSWAYS, written at a later period.

The question remains, what comfort is there in voluntary escape? The poems which most directly answer this question are another pair of companion poems, "The Indian to His Love" and "The Falling of the Leaves" (with "Ephemera" as a kind of postscript). As in the shepherd poems, the first of these represents the innocence of dream, and the second reveals the disillu-

sionment of reality that follows closely thereafter. In the first
poem the Indian and his beloved stroll along the shore of their
island paradise, imagining a future of perfect bliss uninterrupted
even by death. But despite the splendor of the setting, the poet
plants in the final two stanzas certain suggestions that their idyll
cannot endure. In the third stanza, for example, the Indian
reflects:

> How we alone of mortals are
> Hid under quiet boughs apart,
> While our love grows an Indian star,
> A meteor of the burning heart,
> One with the tide that gleams, the wings
>   that gleam and dart.

The comparison of their love to the meteor prophesies the waning of passion which is revealed in the following poem. Their love
is indeed one with the tide that ebbs and with the wings that
glide away and are gone. In the final stanza these prophetic
hints of disillusionment are reinforced by others. The first stanza's
"great boughs [that] drop tranquillity" become merely "heavy"
boughs; and instead of the opening stanza's peahens dancing on
a smooth lawn, there is the burnished dove "That moans and
sighs a hundred days."

The poem ends with a startling juxtaposition of fire and water,
which injects energy into what is otherwise a static though richly
conceived poem:

> How when we die our shades will rove,
> When eve has hushed the feathered ways,
> With vapoury footsole by the water's drowsy blaze.

The overall languorous quality of the idyll virtually extinguishes
the force of this final phrase, unexpected and yet in a certain
sense climactic; the muted violence of "water's drowsy blaze"
suggests once again the impossibility of the lush, romantic stasis
of the idyll. "Blaze" is a powerful word choice for this purpose,

following as it does such lulling modifiers as "hushed," "feathered," "vapoury," and "drowsy." There is even a delicate note of irony in the lover's offering this image while prophesying a future which will not be a future at all, but rather an eventless continuation of the present.

Future has become present in the companion poem, "The Falling of the Leaves," and the pathetic futility of the lover's confident prophecy becomes clear. Long before death the lovers' passion has waned, and the culprit—as one might easily have predicted from the other poem—is time itself. "The hour of the waning of love has beset us / . . . / Let us part, ere the season of passion forget us." Having escaped from the unquiet lands, the lovers find that their deadliest foe is inescapable; as happened earlier, the song of innocence is drowned out by the lament of experience.

Is this, then, the poet of escape? Is this he who sees only a "static universe of moods and dreams"? As Ellmann writes, "When Yeats seriously contemplates leaving the observable world, he customarily points out what a mistake it would be. . . . So far from yielding to another world of the spirit, Yeats in his verse is always demonstrating that we had better cling to this one. . . . He acknowledges the call of isolation, but affirms that he will resist it." [17]

"Ephemera," mentioned earlier as constituting a kind of postscript to the companion poems just discussed, makes an important contribution to the theme of reconciliation. At first it seems to do no more than advance the disintegration of passion a step or two farther in that "hour of gentleness / When the poor tired child, Passion, falls asleep." Again the image of the meteor appears, but whereas in the ardor of early passion the lover had compared his *love* to a meteor, now it is dead leaves which fall "like faint meteors in the gloom." Reinforcing this carefully

17 Ellmann, *The Identity of Years*, x-xi.

structured atmosphere of decline, a rabbit—that ancient symbol of fecundity—appears, old and lame, limping down the path: "Autumn was over him."

Nevertheless, even if the lovers' escape has been doomed from the start because of the inescapability of time, Yeats ends "Ephemera" with an astonishing step toward affirmation and reconciliation—a five-line consolation statement that scarcely seems to belong to the poem at all:

> 'Ah, do not mourn,' he said,
> 'That we are tired, for other loves await us;
> Hate on and love through unrepining hours.
> Before us lies eternity; our souls
> Are love, and a continual farewell.'

There have already been many rudimentary anticipations of the later poetry—the peculiar whirling motions in several CROSS-WAYS poems, for example, suggest the later gyres; the dance motif has appeared; and the dramatic juxtaposition of opposite forces has been there from the first. But here is the first unmistakable antecedent of *A Vision's* system of nearly perpetual cyclic recurrence, bringing renewal ("other loves await us") after each decline. Present also is the noble acceptance of opposite forces ("Hate on and love"), generally considered a characteristic only of Yeats's late poetry. The poem has not dealt with hate in any sense, nor have any of the previous ones; yet here is the poet (or, to be more precise, his persona) warmly recommending both love and hate. It hardly matters that these final lines seem to be tacked arbitrarily and irrelevantly onto a minor poem, for they signal an important step in Yeats's attitude toward experience. The unrelieved restlessness we have seen in the earliest poems, suggesting an idealistic young man's iconoclastic quest for a god worthy of the name, at last yields to a moment of visionary insight into the universal order: "Before us lies eternity; our souls / Are love, and a continual farewell."

Having examined Yeats's earliest treatment of the possibilities of aestheticism and escape into dream, one concludes that neither can reconcile reality with the poet's imaginative image of the ideal, the whole. The CROSSWAYS poems offer a third and final possibility for reconciliation: the sympathy of nature. If some response could be won from the realm of physical nature, some unmistakable evidence of a unity which embraces both man and nature, then the human condition would be more meaningful and consequently more bearable.

In this early period Yeats's attitude toward nature is strikingly reminiscent of Wordsworth's conception of a natural bond between man and nature. But whereas Wordsworth voiced his certainty that such a bond existed, Yeats reveals only an eager willingness to find evidence of a bond. In many of these poems he seems to search eagerly for a sign of nature's participation in some kind of sympathetic harmony with mankind; but on each occasion he is ultimately disappointed. Both Yeats's kinship with and his departure from Wordsworth's attitude toward nature can be illustrated by comparing Yeats's sad shepherd, who roams the countryside seeking comfort from nature and discovers only universal indifference, with the following lines from Wordsworth's "To My Sister":

> Love, now a universal birth,
> From heart to heart is stealing,
> From earth to man, from man to earth:
> —It is the hour of feeling.

It is as if Wordsworth held the key to a secret that Yeats yearned to discover. Always impatient with descriptions of the beauties of physical nature, Yeats manipulates natural imagery—even in his early poetry—for symbolic purposes; and even when he demands answers from nature, he seems too impatient to wait for them, or even to listen for them; thus nature could never become for him as it has been for Wordsworth—"the nurse, / The guide, the guardian of my heart, and soul / Of all my moral being."

As if deliberately to frustrate him, nature seems to toy with man in these early poems, tantalizing him with strange whispers and magical signs, but then failing, finally, to grant him sympathy or a coherent message of any kind. But there is an underlying conviction, nonetheless, that nature *could* speak if she could only be induced to do so. She at least makes many promising sounds. In "The Song of the Happy Shepherd" there is the curious image of the "humming sea," and in "The Sad Shepherd," the similar image of "humming sands." Even more curious is an elaborate metaphor in "Anashuya and Vijaya" in which Yeats describes the stars as Kama's arrows (the equivalent of Cupid's) which pierce the twilight—the arrows being referred to as "murmuring barbs." This is particularly unusual since stars—unlike sea and sand—are for most poets soundless. (As we shall see shortly, in other poems Yeats's stars laugh, sing, and sigh as well as murmur.) The most important and emphatic of such nature sounds, however, comes in "The Madness of King Goll," in which each stanza ends in the haunting refrain, *"They will not hush, the leaves a-flutter round me, the beech leaves old."* This time the message from nature is clear: the king cannot escape the march of time. But like the sea, the sands, and the stars of the previous poems, the leaves are oblivious of man's destiny to grow old and die; they grant him no solace. In fact, one could argue that there is a kind of malevolence—certainly from King Goll's point of view—in the relentlessness of the falling leaves' message. Still there is no real communion between man and nature; rather, man interprets nature as a commentary upon his own mortality. In considering nature's suggestive sounds, we may be reminded once again of the seashell which the happy shepherd promises will transform a tale in "melodious guile," but which instead turns the sad shepherd's whispered words to "inarticulate moan." In all of these poems the realm of physical nature remains utterly remote from the world of men; in view of Yeats's own apparent indifference to the possible uses of nature in poetry, however much he was devoted to the natural beauty of the Sligo countryside, it is less surprising that he found no answers in nature than that he sought them there in the first place.

The most persistent image of nature in the CROSSWAYS poems is the star, which appears with varying importance in eight of the first ten poems; it then seems to have exhausted the poet's interest for the moment, appearing only once again in the remaining six poems. In a sense, Yeats's star is an adequate symbol for all of nature in these poems, for what it reveals is true of other aspects of nature which occur less frequently or less significantly.

The image of the shooting star, or meteor—as we have already seen—occurs three times, each time suggesting the terrible brevity of man's condition: the brevity of human life ("Ephemera"), of love ("The Indian to His Love"), and of all earthly creation ("The Song of the Happy Shepherd"). The last of these poems offers other instances of star imagery as well: the shepherd warns against seeking learning from "the starry men," or astronomers, who follow "The whirling ways of stars that pass"; "the cold star-bane" (which may be read as star-curse or star-poison) has destroyed their "human truth." Though generally considered to represent scientists, these starry men may represent all those who err in looking to nature (in this case, to the stars) for an explanation of universal truths. "The Sad Shepherd," a poem which qualifies and clarifies this first poem in ways already described, substantiates this reading by showing the indifference of nature to man's misery; the stars "Among themselves laugh on and sing alway." Hence the first two CROSSWAYS poems dispute the older Romantic faith in nature as a spiritual guide and revealer of secret truths.

In "Anashuya and Vijaya," the young priestess and her lover offer three separate prayers to the stars, each time asking of them some display of human feeling. The stars are asked to sigh, to sing, and to weep; and after these requests have been made, the central problem of the poem (a love triangle) is interrupted as the two lovers discuss the matter of nature's (or the gods') sympathy with mankind, as exemplified by the stars. "What know the pilots of the stars of tears?" Anashuya asks, and Vijaya answers: "Their faces are all worn, and in their eyes / Flashes the fire of sadness." He then offers reasons for the stars' sadness: they look down upon men frozen in snow, upon icicles famishing the North, and upon prides of lions cowering in flaming forests. Here is the typically Yeatsian vision of opposites—ice and fire. Perhaps we are also meant to observe that all three of these examples demonstrate desolation by natural forces (assuming that the forest fire is of some natural origin). The stars look down—sadly, Vijaya believes—upon the destructive operation of natural laws, the presence of destructive opposites in the created world. In the final speech of the poem, Anashuya has begun to doubt her lover's assertion that the stars grieve for mankind's lot. Though she begins her prayer, "*I have forgiven, O new star!*" she stops short and considers, "*Maybe you have not heard of us.*" Far from sympathizing, perhaps the stars are oblivious of what they seem to gaze upon. Another lady lover shares Anashuya's doubts in "Ephemera": "How far away the stars seem," she remarks, suggesting, perhaps, the blind indifference of nature to the waning of passion which is tormenting her.

The last important use of star imagery in the CROSSWAYS poems occurs in "The Madness of King Goll." As the old king reminisces over the bold and reckless adventures of his youth, he remarks that during one such adventure "stars were blinking"; during another, "keen stars above me shone"; and during a third, "starlight gleamed." The poet seems to stress the steadiness and isolation of these stars, gazing down on the heedless adventurer as he burns himself out of life; and at the end of his days, his spirit broken and glory lost, only the "dying sun" is witness. It may be significant that his youthful adventures occurred at night, while he faces death in bright daylight. From such evidence it seems that if nature shares anything at all with mankind, it is that nature and man are both imprisoned in time, both subject to change and finally death. As with the burning meteors and the short-lived earth, the falling leaves and the waning of passion, the parallel between changing man and changing nature is fairly constant in these early poems.

But man and nature remain apart; there is no bond, no sympathetic response, and for Yeats, in these poems at least, not even the consolation of nature's beauty. He ends the CROSSWAYS poems with "The Ballad of the Foxhunter," in which an old man dies while a young huntsman blows on the horn "A gay wandering cry." At the moment of death a blind hound lifts its head to mourn; and as the body is borne indoors by servants, the other hounds begin wailing for the dead. On the surface, certainly this is no optimistic note for an ending; but the old foxhunter has led a rich, active life: even at death fire is in his eyes, and his fingers "move and sway" to the *gay* music of the horn. Implicit in this presentation is the poet's respect for worldly experience, for aristocratic habit and dignity—the elements of *custom* and *ceremony* which Yeats was to praise thirty years later in "A Prayer for My Daughter." It seems an unlikely poem from a poet accused of turning his back on human experience in favor of dreams and decoration, a starry-eyed, immature aesthete for whom words alone are certain good. The answer, of course, is that even in his earliest poems Yeats gives evidence of the restless and urgent search for lasting values which characterizes his best-known work. Even as a young poet he was never content to make a separate peace, but reached toward expanding insights and the more inclusive vision necessary to embrace a universe of opposites.

2

THE ROSE
and the Quest for
Eternal Beauty

IN THE poems of THE ROSE, the brooding, melancholy searching of CROSSWAYS gives way to a more vigorous and affirmative quest for reconciliation. No longer lamenting the waning of passion and youth and other miseries of mortality, and no longer simply casting about for something better, Yeats announces in the first poem of THE ROSE his confident conviction that there *is* something better: a mystic wisdom which will compensate for all such miseries by revealing them as only a portion of a vast and orderly scheme of creation. His effort to describe that scheme will be recorded only much later in the elaborate machinery of *A Vision*; but THE ROSE commences his determined and aggressive quest for the mystic wisdom which will shape that description.

In THE ROSE the reconciliation of all opposite forces is the anticipated result of Yeats's quest for eternal beauty, a quest which he begins by a deliberate juxtaposition of various antinomies: he will seek the eternal in the ephemeral, the mystic in the commonplace, and the ideal in the real. Whereas in CROSSWAYS such antinomies constituted polar opposites, in THE ROSE

31

they have become intermixed to such a degree that one force is contained within its opposite.

This mixture of opposites, occurring as it does in the observable physical world, indicates at least two important steps forward in Yeats's path toward reconciling opposites. One is the philosophic sophistication that enables him to perceive not merely that the human condition is characterized by the existence of opposite forces such as A and B, but also that A exists within B and that B exists within A, each tempering the other. He is not yet able to schematize this perception through the economical image of interpenetrating cones, but the basic insight is there. The second advance is the poet's firmer grasp of the concrete realities that constitute what he will one day call (in "The Circus Animals' Desertion") the "foul rag-and-bone shop of the heart." As Yeats moves from the basically egocentric search of CROSSWAYS to a more objective and vigorous confrontation with experience, THE ROSE poems show evidence of his keener consciousness of the physical world and its inhabitants. Obviously such an expanded scope is necessary if one seeks reconciliation through a vision of the entire cosmos and its pattern.

The "eternal beauty" which is the object of the poet's newly announced quest is never defined very sharply, either in the poems themselves or in the prose commentaries that Yeats often append-ed to his poems at this stage of his career; but it is clear that the term represents mystical knowledge of a kind that will give the poet superior insight into the harmonious operation of the uni-verse. Beyond the poet's conviction that he can discover such knowledge in the ancient lore of his nation and in the common-place, ephemeral qualities of human life, he claims to know little of its nature. As his quest begins, such ignorance is understand-able, of course, since he has not yet attained his goal. For this reason, when we encounter a difficult poem like "The Rose of Battle," in which the rose / beauty is even more obliquely de-scribed than elsewhere, we should probably regard the haziness as a record of incomplete discovery, as beauty glimpsed incompletely, rather like the partial vision of Plato's cave dweller in the *Republic*. Only three of its qualities are certain from the start: it is eternal, beautiful, and *mystical*—for the knowledge which Yeats seeks is evidently reserved for only the most diligent and imaginative pursuers. He can *"But seek alone to hear the strange things said / By God to the bright hearts of those long dead, / And learn to chaunt a tongue men do not know."*

If eternal beauty is never precisely defined, Yeats creates an even more difficult problem of definition with the rose, which is his primary symbol in this second group of poems.[1] Between Yeats's prose comments, liberally offered over the years, and those of his commentators, the fragile rose of his 1890s verse has been burdened with a gargantuan load of symbolism and has been variously credited with representing, or being related to, the following (among others):

> spiritual love
> eternal beauty
> woman's beauty
> a compound of beauty and peace
> a compound of beauty and wisdom
> Shelley's Intellectual Beauty, altered to
>   sympathize with human suffering
> physical love
> Ireland
> religion
> Maud Gonne
> the sun
> the divine nature
> the flower of the Virgin
> Apuleius's flower (*The Golden Ass*)
> the female impulse toward life (as
>   opposed to the male impulse toward
>   death)

1 THE ROSE was not a separate volume of poems, but was Yeats's heading for a group of poems in the collection *Poems* (London, 1895).

the female generative organs
a key Rosicrucian symbol.

The point of this observation is neither to berate nor to praise the poet for exploiting one symbol in such a formidable variety of associations, but simply to demonstrate that he is safe from the charge of those who see the poet of THE ROSE as a misty-eyed aesthete who is unconcerned with ideas. If we can seldom determine with certainty what the rose is meant to suggest in a particular poem, it is not because the image exists in a vacuum of mere prettiness but rather because it is an ambiguous symbol (though never merely a vague one). If Yeats can be faulted in his intellectual application of the rose symbol, his error may be experimenting too freely with his symbols and ideas; certainly, as the list of associations indicates, he does not *lack* ideas. Always in the proudest sense a traditional poet, he chooses the rose for its accrued richness of association, not for its loveliness alone. As he writes in a note accompanying another volume: "Once a symbolism has possessed the imagination of large numbers of men, it becomes, as I believe, an embodiment of disembodied powers, and repeats itself in dreams and visions, age after age." [2]

Undeniably, the ambiguity resulting from these multiple associations does imperil the reader's apprehension of THE ROSE poems. The accumulated array of "meanings" has a pernicious way of intruding itself between reader and poem so that he may find himself wondering, often despite himself, whether the rose in a particular verse stands for Ireland, for Maud Gonne, or for physical love. Yeats compounded this problem: many years after writing THE ROSE poems, he came to regret much of his early poetry and took to dressing it up by suggesting symbolic associations that had not been intentional at the time of composition.

2 W. B. Yeats, note accompanying "The Valley of the Black Pig," Peter Allt and Russell K. Alspach (eds.), *The Variorum Edition of the Poems of W. B. Yeats* (New York: Macmillan, 1968), 810.

He was particularly fond of discovering symbolic applications of the rose (and other of his images) in ancient literature which he had never previously read, since he felt that such historic associations lent power and tradition to his symbols. Even when he could not identify his sources, he was eager to supply historic precedents: "I am writing away from most of my books," he comments in an explanatory note, "and have not been able to find the passage; but I certainly read it somewhere." [3]

The poet's revisions of the poems further compound this problem, for in giving THE ROSE poems serious attention, one must consider both the original published versions and the frequently very different revised versions. "The Sorrow of Love," to cite one example, became an entirely different poem in 1925, yet it appears in its final form under the 1893 grouping in *The Collected Poems.*

In considering the reconciliation theme, or any other, in THE ROSE poems, one would be wise to restrict the ever-widening suggestiveness of the rose symbol to the one or two meanings (or "qualities") which seem to govern each individual poem. What Yeats said later about the rose, or whatever alternate meanings he may have had in mind when he wrote of it, should probably not concern us here unless the poem itself suggests such variant interpretations. In following this approach one should keep in mind the observation of Ellmann and others, that Yeats's symbols are always inclined to be slippery, so that what the rose "means" in one poem may have little bearing upon its meaning in another.[4] There is, however, one prose definition which Yeats supplies in a note to a later volume, *The Wind Among the Reeds,* which serves admirably as a working definition throughout THE

3 W. B. Yeats, note accompanying "The Secret Rose," Allt and Alspach (eds.), *The Variorum Edition*, 813.
4 Richard Ellmann, *The Identity of Yeats* (New York: Oxford University Press, 1964), xix.

ROSE: "The Rose has been for many centuries a symbol of spiritual love and supreme beauty." [5]

In the opening poem, "To the Rose upon the Rood of Time," Yeats announces his poetic quest and closely identifies the rose with the object of his quest—eternal beauty. He asks the rose to come near so that he may discover eternal beauty, a request which makes it possible to interpret the rose as inspiration or as beauty itself. The latter reading is more satisfactory, I believe; and though it may be argued that rose and beauty are not clearly equated, it may also be argued that they are not clearly distinguished from each other. Certainly no problem arises in reading THE ROSE poems as if the rose and eternal beauty are precisely the same thing, and there is ample critical precedent for doing so. (The rose, in this context, is no longer the ephemeral flower, of course, but a poetic image that apparently has little in common with the actual flower apart from its formal beauty.) As dominant symbol, the rose here reveals the new focus of Yeats's urge toward reconciliation. "Come near," he says to the rose, and for perhaps the first time we can confidently assume that we hear the poet's own voice rather than that of a persona:

> *Come near, that no more blinded by man's fate,*
> *I find under the boughs of love and hate,*
> *In all poor foolish things that live a day,*
> *Eternal beauty wandering on her way.*

The passage is a significant one. The line, *"no more blinded by man's fate,"* suggests that Yeats has at least partially renounced the kind of lamentation he expressed in CROSSWAYS. If human fate cannot be altered, then it must somehow be accepted; and in facing up to the negative side of the human condition, the poet resolves to seek its positive side as well: *"Eternal beauty wandering on her way."*

5 W. B. Yeats, note accompanying "Aedh Pleads With the Elemental Powers," Allt and Alspach (eds.), *The Variorum Edition*, 811.

The first stanza signals an advance in attitude from the CROSS-WAYS poems. The poet promises to sing of *"The Druid, grey, wood-nurtured, quiet-eyed,/ Who cast round Fergus dreams, and ruin untold."* In CROSSWAYS the consolation of dream—in its various forms—was posed as a seductive possibility and then found (by the poet, but not always by his characters) to be inadequate. But here the *peril* of dream is clearly acknowledged, perhaps for the first time in Yeats's poetry, though "The Madness of King Goll" and *The Wanderings of Oisin* offer less distinct examples of the same idea. A certain kind of dream, in this case the attainment of mystical insight, can bring with it "ruin untold." This marks a major step in Yeats's development from a disillusioned idealist toward an impassioned realist who clings persistently to his ideals. It demonstrates the double-edged aspects of the imagination—seductive and yet in a curious way fatal. Edmund Wilson sees this as characteristic of the early poetry: "The world of the imagination is shown us in Yeats's early poetry as something infinitely delightful, infinitely seductive, as something to which one becomes addicted, with which one becomes delirious and drunken—and as something which is somehow incompatible with, and fatal to, the good life of that actual world which is so full of weeping and from which it is so sweet to withdraw."[6]

For the happy CROSSWAYS shepherd, the life of the imagination was merely delusory; for the sad shepherd, it was an unattainable consolation for human misery. But now, for Fergus—a wiser, more formidable figure than either shepherd—imaginative revelation can be even destructive.

This same stanza offers stars which, *"grown old / In dancing silver-sandalled on the sea, / Sing in their high and lonely melody"* of the sadness of the rose. In CROSSWAYS, the worlds of man and nature had seemed completely divorced from each other, and the forces of nature—in particular the stars—were oblivious of man's

6 Edmund Wilson, "W. B. Yeats," in James Hall and Martin Steinmann (eds.), *The Permanence of Yeats* (New York: Macmillan, 1961), 16.

personal tragedies. One must take care not to make too much of this, but now even the stars are subject to the laws of time and change: they have *grown old* in their dance (as the sun did in "King Goll"), and now they sing of the sadness of the rose, which is in turn sad for the sufferings of man. This is not so much an innovation as an interesting shift in relationships, for it suggests a somewhat closer integration of man and nature than the previous poems did. The link between man's suffering and the stars' "*high and lonely melody*" is eternal beauty.

The most important revelation of "To the Rose upon the Rood of Time," however, concerns the two sources from which Yeats expects to discover eternal beauty: Irish folklore and "*all poor foolish things that live a day.*" As mentioned earlier, THE ROSE reveals Yeats's firmer grasp of concrete realities, and this line expresses his dedication to the common components of everyday life—not for their own sake, but rather for what they can show him of eternal beauty. This opening poem is characteristically rich in antinomies: the dream/wisdom and ruin just described, the "*boughs of love and hate*" wherein the rose grows, and now the expectation of discovering what is eternal in what is ephemeral. Clearly the antinomies, too, will play a major role in the poems here introduced. David Daiches observes the persistence of dichotomies such as these in Yeats's early work: "We note in these early poems a general tendency to construct a pattern in terms of a simple pair of contrasts. Human activity as opposed to fairy activity, the natural as opposed to the artificial, the familiar as opposed to the remote and strange, the domestic as opposed to the heroic, the contemporary as opposed to the ancient, the transient as opposed to the permanent—these contrasts provide nearly all the themes in *Crossways* and *The Rose*." [7]

This dedication to the ordinary is admirable, especially in so young and idealistic a poet, for it reveals a sense of largeness that

7 David Daiches, "W. B. Yeats—I," in Hall and Steinmann (eds.), *The Permanence of Yeats*, 117.

is rooted in the commonplace even as it reaches out for what is eternal. It also reflects an important awareness of the paradoxes that would occupy Yeats in his most highly praised work of later years. Less admirable, according to some observers (specifically Harold Bloom), is Yeats's entreaty, repeated six times in the poem, for the rose to *"come near."* As Bloom says: "The Rose is to come near, but to leave him still 'a little space' for the natural odor of less occult roses to pervade. Come near, but not too near; this is the start of a characteristic pattern of vacillation." [8]

Pity the hapless poet: when he espouses his cause too wholeheartedly, he is accused, as Yeats was by those who objected to his mystical studies, of fanaticism; and when he qualifies his intentions, he is chastised for vacillation. Bloom has not recognized in these lines the young Yeats's attempt to solve a problem which every artist must eventually confront—the discovery and maintenance of an ideal aesthetic distance from his material (including his own private ideas and opinions). Come near, but not too near—is this vacillation, or is it rather the rapidly maturing artist's recognition of the need to stand slightly apart from his own causes, to satisfy, in short, the requirement for artistic balance. In this case it seems appropriate for Yeats to qualify as he does his entreaty to the rose:

> *Ah, leave me still*
> *A little space for the rose-breath to fill!*
> *Lest I no more hear common things that crave.*

He must not allow himself to be so completely consumed by the fire of beauty that he neglects its humble sources, nor must he become so engrossed in the commonplace that he loses sight of the beauty he seeks there. It seems to me that the poem is essentially *about* the need for balance in the new quest to which the poet is committing himself. There must be no more of his being blinded

8 Harold Bloom, *Yeats* (New York: Oxford University Press, 1970), 111.

by the uglier truths of man's fate, no more futile lamentation, but rather a search for reconciliation and fulfillment in eternal beauty. This is a positive step and—since this lofty poetic quest is grounded in everyday experience—even a peculiarly practical one. Far from vacillating, Yeats has not only made up his mind that the rose must approach him, he has also settled on the appropriate distance that must exist between them! Unterecker defends the passage similarly in discussing the occult symbolism of THE ROSE: "Yeats's prayer, in the opening poem's second stanza, that the rose breath come near but that it not engulf him is therefore a prayer that he be allowed to function at the intersecting point, that point at which—mortal but in touch with immortal things— he is able to hold fixed in mind on Time's destructive cross the Rose, symbol of imperishable order." [9]

In its dedication to ordinary experience, "To the Rose upon the Rood of Time" has much in common with the much later and more famous poem, "The Circus Animals' Desertion," which concludes:

> Now that my ladder's gone,
> I must lie down where all the ladders start,
> In the foul rag-and-bone shop of the heart.

As yet incapable of such powerful imagery, the young Yeats seems nonetheless to suggest a ladder of a kind, one which will proceed from *"The weak worm hiding down in its small cave"* and *"The field-mouse running by me in the grass"* to *"mortal hopes that toil and pass,"* and from there to the higher wisdom of *"the strange things said / By God to the bright hearts of those long dead."* At the top of this approximation of a neo-Platonic ladder, the poet expects to be able to *"chaunt a tongue men do not know,"* having ascended from the lowliest of observations (the worm and the mouse) to those which surpass the normal

9 John Unterecker, *A Reader's Guide to William Butler Yeats* (New York: Noonday Press, 1959), 76.

boundaries of human understanding. Yeats himself mentions a ladder in association with the Tree of Life (upon which he imagines the rose to be growing) in an explanatory note to a later poem:

I once stood beside a man in Ireland when he saw [*the Rose*] growing there in a vision, that seemed to have rapt him out of his body. He saw the garden of Eden walled about, and on the top of a high mountain . . . he came to a tall, dark tree, with little bitter fruits, and was shown a kind of stair or ladder going up through the tree, and told to go up; and near the top of the tree, a beautiful woman, like the Goddess of Life associated with the tree in Assyria, gave him a rose that seemed to have been growing upon the tree.[10]

The man's vision seems to have had considerable effect upon Yeats's own poetic visions; for this steady ascent, ending in the bestowing of a rose, is so similar to Yeats's quest as to serve as a gloss to the poem under discussion and to the quest of THE ROSE. Yeats always associates eternal beauty in these poems with a beautiful woman, and mystical knowledge seems always to await the poet like a reward on high. It is a noble task Yeats set for himself in this poem, and a noble introduction to the poems that follow.

THE ROSE poems display impressive evidence of Yeats's success in mining the commonplace and ancient folklore in search of mystical insight into eternal beauty. Especially as compared to the CROSSWAYS poems, these reveal fresh insights on the part of the poet's characters and the poet as well. Second, they contain a new and vigorous dramatic energy, as evidenced by such elements as direct confrontation, dialogue, closeness of the teller to the tale, and spontaneous insights of a kind lacking in most earlier poems. Third, there is a remarkable advance in rendering physical gesture and other description, which indicates Yeats's closer

10 W. B. Yeats, note accompanying "Aedh Pleads with the Elemental Powers," Allt and Alspach (eds.), *The Variorum Edition*, 811.

observation of his environment and increased ability to transform it into poetry.

The surest sign of progress toward mystical wisdom is the arrival of fresh insight. In CROSSWAYS most of the characters were able to perceive nothing more about the nature of their fates than the fact that they were made unhappy; in particular, those who sought some form of consolation were unable to discover it. Practically the sole exception in CROSSWAYS is the Indian lover ("Ephemera") who manages to reach an impressive though limited insight when he looks forward to future incarnations. Instead of seeing in retrospect that his idyllic dreamland by the sea was a hopeless venture from the start, he merely looks ahead to a new chance, through reincarnation, at realizing the same old dream. His moment of vision ("Before us lies eternity; our souls / Are love, and a continual farewell"), striking though it may be, is not equal to those we shall find in THE ROSE. Other CROSSWAYS characters—in "The Indian upon God," "The Ballad of Moll Magee," and "To an Isle in the Water," for instance—are able only to perceive the existing situation, or to dream of a better one, without penetrating the here-and-now to arrive at an understanding equal to the poet's.

In THE ROSE the gap between the characters' viewpoints and that of the poet begins rapidly to close. The characters gain spontaneous insight into their situations, insight equal to what we take to be the poet's own view of their situations. In other cases there is an absence of an identifiable mask, and the reader feels safe (as he never could in CROSSWAYS) in assuming that the speaker is not a character at all, but the poet himself. An example of spontaneous insight is seen in "Fergus and the Druid," when Fergus views a parade of his previous incarnations and immediately perceives the great loss that his new wisdom has cost him:

> But now I have grown nothing, knowing all.
> Ah! Druid, Druid, how great webs of sorrow
> Lay hidden in the small slate-coloured thing.

In "Cuchulain's Fight with the Sea" the poet confronts us with the instant of painful revelation—when Cuchulain learns that the man he has just fatally wounded is his own son:

> 'Speak before your breath is done.'
> 'Cuchulain I, mighty Cuchulain's son.'
> 'I put you from your pain. I can no more.'

The terrible moment exists without commentary, without a note of what would have been unnecessary description, so that these final words of the father to his son bear a noble dignity worthy of Sophocles. This kind of immediate and painful confrontation, so terrible that the life of the person who experiences it is marked ever after, shows not only an increase in Yeats's sense of dramatic force, but also a more dynamic energy than was shown in the most energetic of the CROSSWAYS poems.

"The Ballad of Father Gilligan" offers examples of direct confrontation, spontaneous insight, and increased dramatic energy. The weary old priest, having fallen asleep after being summoned to a dying man, awakes and rushes to the man's bedside:

> 'And is the poor man dead?' he cried.
> 'He died an hour ago.'
> The old priest Peter Gilligan
> In grief swayed to and fro.

But the widow reports that her husband died only shortly after Father Gilligan's earlier visit; and the priest (who has in fact made no earlier visit) realizes that God has sent an angel to represent him:

> 'He Who is wrapped in purple robes,
> With planets in His care,
> Had pity on the least of things
> Asleep upon a chair.'

The little ballad is not one of Yeats's most memorable poems, but it does show some interesting changes since the CROSSWAYS

ballad about another priest, "The Ballad of Father O'Hart."
Father O'Hart's story, told by a remote reporter some time after
his death, had no dialogue except for a three-word quotation. In
the later poem, which is not necessarily superior but shows Yeats's
path of development, the poet has moved much closer to his
material. The narration is more personal, more direct, as indicated by the frequency of lively dialogue and by the closeness of
the reporter to the action in both time and sympathy. Moreover,
the theme of "Father Gilligan" seems distinctly suited to the
other poems in THE ROSE, for the priest identifies himself in the
passage quoted above with "the least of things"—an appropriate
instance of Yeats's dedication to the ordinary in "To the Rose
upon the Rood of Time."

Obviously Yeats's determination to discover beauty in the
humblest places is off to a promising start. He is not quite up to
the rustic dimensions of his commitment to observe "The field-
mouse running by me in the grass," perhaps, but he has journeyed
from the comparative remoteness of the CROSSWAYS poems.

Another improvement which is evidence of his success is his
more dramatic rendering of gesture and other physical description. Yeats was able to rise to magnificent description a few times
in CROSSWAYS, as in "The Song of the Happy Shepherd" when
he speculated that the earth may be

> Only a sudden flaming word
> In clanging space a moment heard,
> Troubling the endless reverie.

Another example, almost as effective, was the parrot who "sways
upon a tree, / Raging at his own image in the enamelled sea."
But the scarcity of such examples in CROSSWAYS suggests that
the poet had caught only occasional glimpses of the actual world
around him; but he had won a steadier, more intense vision by
the time he wrote THE ROSE poems. Compare, for example, the
economy and force of the "bee-loud glade" (from "The Lake

Isle of Innisfree") with anything in CROSSWAYS, or the final lines
of "To Some I Have Talked with by the Fire":

> . . . till the morning break
> And the white hush end all but the loud beat
> Of their long wings, the flash of their white feet.

In CROSSWAYS physical gestures and other descriptive passages
tend to conform to one of two patterns: either a flattened, unconvincing quality, as if the poet were drawing too glibly upon
things he had read or only casually observed; or a rather self-
conscious effort to impose a quasimystical, or at the very least
mysterious, significance upon them.

Representative of the first pattern are the descriptions of hair,
an image that would hold an obvious fascination for Yeats for
many years to come, climaxing in the two dozen or so references
to hair in *The Wind Among the Reeds.* Hair is mentioned several
times in CROSSWAYS, usually only casually; but in "The Madness
of King Goll" it serves as a metaphor in the line, "Orchil shakes
out her long dark hair," suggesting the approach of night. Orchil,
Yeats tells us in a note, is a Fomorian sorceress (". . . if I remember rightly. I forget whatever I may have once known about
her.")[11] who represents the powers of death, darkness, cold, and
evil. But the line, evidently meant to be especially powerful,
succeeds neither as metaphor nor as a convincing image. With
its heavily accented feet, the line is minimally expressive—as if
the poet were making an obligatory nod to some remote Romantic tradition that has women or goddesses shake out their hair.
The meter more nearly suggests the stamping of feet. In "Anashuya and Vijaya" we find the unsettling image of two deceased
spirits, "A little from the other shades apart, / With mingling
hair." If less prosaic than the first example, this one is certainly
more awkward, for it suggests too literally a tangling of locks

---

11 W. B. Yeats, note accompanying "The Madness of King Goll," Allt
and Alspach (eds.), *The Variorum Edition,* 796.

rather than a blissful union in the afterlife. Certainly neither of these examples approaches the evocative phrase from "The Rose of Battle": "With blown, spray-dabbled hair." This image enchants the reader's ear as well as his eye.

Sometimes the descriptions in CROSSWAYS bear a vague, mystical suggestiveness that seldom seems to work as the poet intends. The stars, for example, get so much descriptive attention in "Anashuya and Vijaya" that they must be considered integral to the poem's structure; but unless we generously assume that Yeats planned to use the stars more significantly in the unwritten final portion of the poem, we must acknowledge that they serve primarily as a form of cluttered decoration. Perhaps it would have been wiser to present the stars merely as stars, so that when Anashuya prays to them they could—by being stars rather than divinities—suggest the utter hopelessness of her prayer; instead, the poet suggests that they are divinities deaf to human entreaties, and the stars inspire a variety of complicated, incompatible metaphors:

ANASHUYA: *Sigh, O you little stars! O sigh and shake your blue*
             apparel!
VIJAYA: *. . . Kama . . .*
           Rises, and showers abroad his fragrant arrows,
           Piercing the twilight with their murmuring barbs.
         . . . .
              O first few stars,
          Whom Brahma . . . praises, for you hold
          The van of wandering quiet . . .
         . . . .
          Sing, till you raise your hands and sigh, and from
            your carheads peer,
          *With all your whirling hair, and drop many an **azure tear**.*
ANASHUYA: What know the pilots of the stars of tears?
VIJAYA: Their faces are all worn, and in their eyes
           Flashes the fire of sadness . . .
         . . . .

ANASHUYA: *You hunter of the fields afar!*
. . . .
Shoot on him shafts of quietness. . . .

Thus in a single poem the stars are (1) sighing little creatures
garbed in blue; (2) the barbs of a god's arrows; (3) holders of
the "van of wandering quiet"; (4) singing, sighing, weeping creatures with hands, peering from carheads; (5) some sort of guided
missile requiring pilots; (6) worn-faced creatures with eyes of
fire (which would seem to be equivalents of the stars themselves);
and (7) hunters armed with arrows. Most readers are likely to
dismiss such murky imagery with a shudder in favor of the
majestic yet economical image of stars in the final line of "Who
Goes with Fergus":

> For Fergus rules the brazen cars,
> And rules the shadows of the wood,
> And the white breast of the dim sea
> And all dishevelled wandering stars.

Descriptions of people, too, become more vivid in THE ROSE.
Yeats, no doubt influenced by ancient Irish legends, chooses to
describe the lover in "Down by the Salley Gardens" (from CROSS-
WAYS) in peculiarly wraithlike terms: "She passed the salley
gardens with little snow-white feet," and "on my leaning shoulder
she laid her snow-white hand." In retrospect, it seems easy to
forgive the young man in the poem for not following the advice
of such a grim and lifeless figure, who seems not so much a
beatific vision of womanhood as a victim of disease. This is almost
the sole description of a person in the entire volume. Compare it
to the Druid in "Fergus and the Druid," who describes himself
thus to Fergus:

> Look on my thin grey hair and hollow cheeks
> And on these hands that may not lift the sword,
> This body trembling like a wind-blown reed.

The difference in richness and energy is all the more impressive when we remember that the two poems were published only six years apart.

Dramatic and convincing gestures are another sign of the descriptive power Yeats demonstrates in THE ROSE. Richest of all these poems in gesture is "Cuchulain's Fight with the Sea," which vividly creates the formidable, vigorous figure of Emer:

> Then Emer cast the web upon the floor,
> And raising arms all raddled with the dye,
> Parted her lips with a loud sudden cry.
>
> . . . .
> 'You dare me to my face,' and thereupon
> She smote with raddled fist, and where her son
> Herded the cattle came with stumbling feet.

Among the CROSSWAYS poems, gesture, like physical description, is rare; the figures appear and move in an abstract pattern, like the impersonal, stylized figures in an ancient fairy tale. One of the few precise physical gestures in that volume appears in "Anashuya and Vijaya," and—not surprisingly—it is metaphorical rather than literal: "The sun has laid his chin on the grey wood, / Weary, with all his poppies gathered round him." This gesture is cloyingly quaint, like metaphors in children's verse where suns and moons behave like human beings. Certainly the sun's gesture does not compare with the descriptions of Emer, "raddling raiment in her dun," who raises her arms "all raddled with the dye" and later strikes a messenger "with raddled fist"—forcing the reader three times to see the red ocher dye stains on her hands and arms. The image functions not only visually, but thematically as well; for shortly Emer will send her son out to be killed, and she will have his blood upon her hands.

With new emphasis upon the present, and a fresh application of the past, THE ROSE again represents a shift in direction from CROSSWAYS. This second volume demonstrates another step toward the reconciliation of opposites through the poet's embracing more and more of human experience—in this case a new

dimension of time—to counterbalance his inexperience and idealistic remoteness from the world of men. The opening poems of
the two volumes indicate the difference. "The Song of the Happy
Shepherd" begins with a regretful reflection upon what has been
lost and what wrongs are now practiced:

> The woods of Arcady are dead,
> And over is their antique joy;
> Of old the world on dreaming fed;
> Grey Truth is now her painted toy.

"To the Rose upon the Rood of Time," as we have seen, begins
with preparations for a new poetic commitment, through which
the past will be examined primarily to discover what is timeless—
that is, to serve the present:

> *Red Rose, proud Rose, sad Rose of all my days!*
> *Come near me, while I sing the ancient ways.*

The settings for THE ROSE poems are frequently the mythological past, as in "Fergus and the Druid," but the past seems alive
and real as it never was in the relatively misty backward glances
of CROSSWAYS. The poem just named, for example, presents a
mythological incident entirely in dialogue so that the past is rendered as dramatically as any poem set in the present. Another
mythological poem, "Cuchulain's Fight with the Sea," presents
Emer, who is the most fully realized character in either of the
two groups of poems.

That the reinvigorated past serves a present purpose (a forward-
looking one, at that) is clear not only in the opening poem, but
also in the closing one, "To Ireland in the Coming Times":

> *While still I may, I write for you,*
> *The love I lived, the dream I knew.*
> *From our birthday, until we die,*
> *Is but the winking of an eye;*
> . . . .
> *I cast my heart into my rhymes,*

That you, in the dim coming times,
May know how my heart went with them
After the red-rose-bordered hem.

Just as imagination confronts experience in THE ROSE, so does
the eternal confront the ephemeral, and the mystical the mundane;
but in three of these poems there is the confrontation with *self*,
which is crucial to Yeats's quest for mystic wisdom. Fergus confronts the truth of his own condition in "Fergus and the Druid,"
in which he wins from the Druid a vision of all his previous incarnations and realizes the loss which this vision has cost him.
This poem applies the theory of the previous poem—that beauty
and wisdom can be discovered in the commonplace and in ancient lore—in a distinctively subjective way, or (to borrow terminology from *A Vision*) in an *antithetical* as opposed to a
primary way. Fergus' vision offers at once a review of the commonplace (embodiments of his own self in such ephemeral, ordinary incarnations as "A green drop in the surge, a gleam of light /
Upon a sword, a fir-tree on a hill, / An old slave grinding at a
heavy quern") and a review of the ancient lore of Ireland (the
myth of Fergus' abdication). In another sense Fergus' vision is
uncommon because it is a vision, and common because what it
contains is common. Mystic insight into the ordinary, which
Fergus gains, is the object of the poet's own quest. (The wisdom
which the vision imparts—that Fergus becomes "nothing, knowing all"—will be further discussed below.)

A second confrontation with self occurs in "Cuchulain's Fight
with the Sea" when the mighty warrior Cuchulain slays a young
man and learns too late that his victim is his own son. The line
in which the dying victim identifies himself ("Cuchulain I, mighty
Cuchulain's son") was originally written, "I am Finmole, mighty
Cuchulain's son," and remained thus from 1892 until it was
revised to its present form in 1924. The revision is a happy one
for several reasons, the least being the removal of the ludicrous
name "Finmole" from the poem, and the most important being

the adoption of the father's own name. Perhaps Yeats chose to emphasize this confrontation of the father with his younger self by giving the son the name Cuchulain; certainly that is the effect of the revision. In "Fergus and the Druid" a man of action renounces his throne in order to seek insight, which arrives through a vision. Cuchulain, too, is a man of action; but his own destructive moment of insight comes when he least expects and least desires it. Perhaps such a confrontation is inevitable, forcing one to come to terms with himself whether willingly or not. "But now I have grown nothing, knowing all," the enlightened Fergus says; and Cuchulain, knowing less than all, but a great deal more, is last seen battling courageously but hopelessly with "the invulnerable tide." In the original version the last two lines were: "For four days warred he with the bitter tide, / And the waves flowed above him and he died." In the early version he, like Fergus, had "grown nothing." But even in the revised form his wrestling with the tide displays at once his enormous strength and his utter helplessness. Once again the poet pursues mystic wisdom in the ancient myths, and once again the wisdom gained is in a peculiar sense destructive. To see oneself is much desired; but to see oneself is, ironically, to destroy oneself.

This curious destructive element in self-knowledge climaxes in the third confrontation with self, which appears in one of the most complex poems in the volume, "The Two Trees." The poem has two long parallel stanzas; in the first the poet advises his beloved to gaze into her own heart, where the "holy tree" is growing, and he describes the tree; in the second he warns her to "Gaze no more in the bitter glass," where there are "Broken boughs and blackened leaves." The series of images in the two stanzas correspond closely to each other; and, as Unterecker observes, "Only in name are there two trees. Their images, placed back to back, form one design."[12] But the poet himself favors

12 Unterecker, *A Reader's Guide*, 86.

subjective truth once again, the truth of the heart and the imagination, rather than the ugly image of the mirror, with its "ravens of unresting thought" and "barrenness." Thought thus opposes imagination; and flesh, spirit; and Yeats announces his commitment to the latter of each group. "The Two Trees" reinforces the point Yeats's shepherd made in the first poem of CROSSWAYS. "There is no truth / Saving in thine own heart"; but this poem also qualifies the earlier one by acknowledging—though with horror—the other side of the dual image, the darkened, barren world of decay and death. Truth is indeed subjective, and one must seek it within oneself, not in the terrible mirror of the physical world; but the poet faces up to the double-edged truth of eternal beauty: the trees blend into one design, positive and negative. The all-inclusive vision of the late poems and *A Vision* is hereby one step nearer.

If vision is the object of the quest, loss of energy—resulting in spiritual stagnation—is its enemy, as shown clearly in "Fergus and the Druid." At first Fergus abounds in energy, curiosity, and courage; like the poet, he pushes toward new wisdom despite its peril. He has ample and convincing warning before he puts on this new knowledge. The Druid offers himself as evidence: his hands that cannot (or at least *may* not) lift the sword, his body trembling like a reed, unwanted by woman, unneeded by man. But still Fergus insists that he open the "little bag of dreams," just as the poet, insatiable, thirsts for mystic wisdom. Five lines that were omitted from the poem after its early printing show more fully, though less dramatically, the terrible stagnation that results from the opening of the "small, slate-coloured thing":

> The sorrows of the world bow down my head
> And in my heart the daemons and the gods
> Wage an eternal battle, and I feel
> The pain of wounds, the labour of the spear,
> But have no share in loss or victory.

The obvious lesson is that power and wisdom cannot coexist; Yeats broadens his early use of dream here to show the see-sawing motion of the relationship between the opposite qualities, power and dream insight—first one, then the other, but never the two together. Somehow—and the "how" is an issue that was to occupy Yeats for the rest of his life—the power and the insight destroy each other, hence the "dreams and ruin untold" of "To the Rose upon the Rood of Time." But the poem says much more than this. Implied in Fergus' despairing consciousness of his loss is the poet's own dread of a kind of equipoise which is merely meaningless stasis. The poem suggests that by stepping apart from the warring contraries of our existence (as Fergus does by gaining hidden knowledge) we are left with nothing at all. Is the point of perfect balance between human ignorance and divine wisdom, between such contraries as love and hate, merely a vacuum, a nothingness? Fergus' supernatural insight into all that he has been leaves him nothing. There is a lingering terror in the poem, resounding from the final two lines, which were absent from its first edition:

> Ah! Druid, Druid, how great webs of sorrow
> Lay hidden in the small, slate-coloured thing!

(It is an amusing commentary upon the eagerness of Yeats's critics to see him as an escapist that Louis MacNeice sees this poem as evidence of Yeats's "nostalgia for another world, for a dreamworld which is all knowledge and no action." [13] It is, of course, precisely this condition—knowledge and no action—which distresses the poet and Fergus as well.)

Stagnation, then, is the terrible risk inherent in pushing toward secret knowledge. This theme occurs again in the difficult and generally ignored poem, "The Rose of Battle," which is third in the series that includes "The Rose of the World" and "The Rose of Peace." These poems should be discussed in the order of their appearance, however, for they present still another dialectic—the

13 Louis MacNeice, *The Poetry of W. B. Yeats* (New York: Oxford University Press, 1941), 74.

destructive and beneficent aspects of eternal beauty. If one must suffer in climbing the highest mountain on which the Tree of Life grows, and suffer further in climbing the ladder leading to the top of that tree, he not only gains at last the secret rose, but also receives it from the hand of a beautiful woman. Mystic wisdom of Fergus' kind is not the only aspect of eternal beauty, after all; the beautiful woman is inextricably associated with it.

The beautiful woman reveals in "The Rose of the World" the destructive aspect of eternal beauty; just as mystic wisdom imperils the mind, so does her magnificent beauty imperil the body of the beholder. For a woman's red lips "Troy passed away in one high funeral gleam, and Usna's children died." In acknowledging this terrible power, however, the poet does not really lament it; for perhaps it is just that the world should humble itself, in fire and ashes if necessary, before the altar of beauty. Only the first of the three stanzas describes destructiveness, and even there the reader is led to imagine the magnificence of such women as Helen and Deirdre whose beauty made them capable of causing such devastation. The second stanza reflects upon the permanence of beauty, apotheosizing and impersonalizing the woman into abstraction:

> We and the labouring world are passing by:
> Amid men's souls, that waver and give place
> . . . .
> Lives on this lonely face

And the third (and final) stanza asks the archangels themselves to bow down before such beauty, for God has made the whole world "to be a grassy road / Before her wandering feet." Beauty, created before the world began, shares in divinity.

Before we move on to the beneficent aspect of beauty, as presented in "The Rose of Peace," it may be worthwhile to mention another aspect which stands apart from the pairs of antinomies, but seems to be constant in Yeats's poetry—namely, the unpredictable, whimsical appearances of beauty among men. In the passage just quoted the poet describes beauty's feet as *wandering*, and in the same poem he describes her as mournful, lonely, weary, and kind, a divine being who wanders gently and sadly through the world of men inspiring all men, rather like a catalyst. The word *wandering* was long a favorite of Yeats's; it appears over a dozen times in CROSSWAYS and THE ROSE.

"The Rose of Peace" suggests that if Michael the archangel were to look down upon beauty (as embodied in a beautiful woman), he would abandon the war of heaven with hell and "weave out of the stars / A chaplet for [her] head," so that warfare would cease and there would be "a rosy peace, / A peace of Heaven with Hell." But as Unterecker cautions, the key word is the first word of the poem—*If*.[14] In fact heaven and earth have not humbled themselves before the awesome presence of beauty, and the strife of all warring antinomies continues. The fear of stagnation that colors the final stanza of "Fergus and the Druid" seems to bear a subtle influence upon this poem, too, as if Yeats were almost relieved that such a balance as he described has not been attained—as if he were convinced already that only in the violent warring of contraries can there be life and progress. It is tempting to look ahead to *A Vision*, where Yeats concludes that there can be no life at those two moon phases at which the moon completely absorbs the sun and the sun completely absorbs the moon. "A rosy peace" may negatively imply artificiality.

One must be careful, however, not to burden such a light and elegant poem with too portentous a message. "The Rose of Peace" is taken perhaps too seriously by many of its critics; on the surface it is an extravagant compliment to a beautiful woman, evidently Maud Gonne; and only when the reader transcends this level does he see that the poet's exaggeration serves truth. To ignore the compliment in order to explore that truth is an injustice to the

14 Unterecker, *A Reader's Guide*, 79.

poem, for both levels must be treated as related. Another reason for not taking the poem too seriously is that the relative clumsiness of a couple of phrases suggests that Yeats spent no great labors in writing it. The lines—"Saying all things were well" and "Would come at last to God's great town"—lack the distinctive power he was able to invest in such workaday expressions when he meant to.

At this point, then, Yeats stands in awe of the beautiful, and his awe extends even to those grimmer, destructive aspects exemplified in the waywardness of Helen and Deirdre and other beautiful women of the mythological past. But the question of whether eternal beauty is primarily beneficent or destructive or (as appears to be the case) a fusion of both is not Yeats's most urgent concern, as we see in the third and final poem of the group, "The Rose of Battle." In this poem, more ambitious and considerably more complex than either "The Rose of the World" or "The Rose of Peace," the poet considers eternal beauty in a different aspect—that of love—and represents it as strangely inescapable, as having power over all men, loved and unloved alike, so that it commands respect just as a deity does, whether wrathful or benign.

"The Rose of Battle" deserves close examination, for it poses intricate problems pertaining to the poet's quest for wisdom and ultimate reconciliation. It is, in fact, a knotty problem of a poem, and one that has attracted few commentators. Though the reliable Unterecker, admirable for his clarity and simplicity in the *Reader's Guide* to Yeats, pays it more notice than most do, even he skims past it with disappointing casualness: "Yeats generously excludes happy lovers from the necessary wars, leaving those wars to his unhappy lovers, 'The sad, the lonely, the insatiable,' poets and occultists, who will, waging God's battles, penetrate the mystery of Old Night. Mortal, they will necessarily go down to defeat; but they will have experienced revelation."[15] Although these comments are helpful, the poem is not so simple.

A paraphrase may be useful. Ships prepare to sail to war, and passengers—fearful or hopeful—gather. The poet advises those who hear love sing constantly to stay home, for danger holds no refuge and war no peace for them. Instead, those should sail who have never heard love sing, or who heard it sing but briefly. Those, too, should sail who seek more than earthly wisdom, for it is to these—the sad, lonely, and insatiable—that night reveals her mysteries, and it is these whom God beckons, through their hearts' cry, to wage His wars. Thus manned, the ships loose their sails and wait; later, defeated in war, they will sink; and the cry of the heart—that can neither live nor die—will be heard no more.

The poet described two kinds of men in the poem—those who have found unceasing love, and those who are sad, lonely, or insatiable. One of several curious problems with the poem is that those in the first category would not seem to *need* to seek refuge in danger or peace in war. Yet they seem to be among those who gather, "hushed from fear, or loud with hope," by the ships:

> Turn if you may from battles never done,
> I call, as they go by me one by one,
> Danger no refuge holds, and war no peace,
> For him who hears love sing and never cease,
> Beside her clean-swept hearth, her quiet shade.

It is possible, perhaps, to read the lines to mean that men who have found love have no need to go to war, unlike those who lack love. But the third and fourth lines above seem to suggest that even those who are loved need refuge, and need peace, but cannot hope to find it in war. It is as if they are somehow smothered by love, forced into some unwelcome stasis by the "clean-swept

15 *Ibid.*

hearth" and "quiet shade," so that their spiritual selves are extinguished, and their finer thirsts can never be satisfied. Certainly
the poem dismisses those who are unceasingly loved in favor of
those with whom the poet seems to number himself—"*The sad,
the lonely, the insatiable*," though whether they are dismissed en-
viously or condescendingly (as being not quite fine enough for
spiritual quests) is a moot question. It is strongly tempting, even
if not altogether justified by evidence in the poem, to interpret
this passage as a forerunner of Yeats's later conviction that lack
of personal fulfillment offers a spur to the imagination, so that
he—for example—might never have written his finest poetry had
Maud Gonne consented to marry him. No matter how he dismisses the group who hear "*love sing and never cease*," he states
explicitly that it is to the other group that " *Old Night shall all
her mystery tell.*"

Unterecker believes that those unsatisfied beings who wage
God's battles "will necessarily go down to defeat; but they will
have experienced revelation." It is true that the first part of the
poem implies that this group may succeed in finding refuge in
danger or peace in war. But in fact they cannot, for the ships do
not even travel to God's wars; instead, they "loose thought-woven
sails and wait," evidently for the wars to come to them.

> And when at last, defeated in His wars,
> They have gone down under the same white stars,
> We shall no longer hear the little cry
> Of our sad hearts, that may not live nor die.

Why do the ships loose their sails, and how does the battle
come to them? One clue may lie in the sails that are twice described as "thought-woven." The sails "flap unfurled / Above
the tide of hours" instead of billowing out and stretching taut as
they must in order to move with the wind. Perhaps sails made
from mere intellection are insufficient equipment for a quest for
Old Night's mysteries.

If we make a crude diagram of the poem, we may observe, first of all, that there are two directions of motion described: (1) the horizontal motion of the ships' setting out from shore, leaving behind love's "clean-swept hearth" and "quiet shade" in pursuit of God's battles, presumably located on an opposite shore; and (2) the vertical motion of the ships' sinking, after a period of motionlessness, beneath the high stars. The interruption in the horizontal progress of the ships suggests a correction in favor of vertical progress—from that of mere intellect to the *imaginative* pursuit of mystical knowledge. Twice the water is "dim" and once "grey." The ship is "grey" as well, but the stars above are "white." What is below is indistinct, and what is above is clearer, purer. The "bell that calls us on; the sweet far thing," also described as God's bell, beckons by way of the heart's own cry.

Risky as it may be to set up allegorical equivalents, they may prove helpful. The sea, dim and grey and "sad" (a word used five times in the poem), suggests—as it often does in Yeats's poetry—a chaos which must be crossed, "ravelled" (as it is described in "The Man who Dreamed of Faeryland") as opposed to the "woven" isle or the "woven" sails. This is the chaotic worldly environment through which a life proceeds. The ship suggests both the archetypal mystical quest and a single soul's progress through life. The sails represent mere thought, as opposed to imagination, and are therefore inadequate. The sinking of the ships suggests death, but only of the body; for even though the cry of the heart (God's bell, the bell buoy which guides the ship safely on its path) no longer sounds, it is not dead. The problem is that it is not alive, either, for it "may not live nor die." The poem ends, not in the triumph of revelation before death, as Unterecker says, but rather in a failure to achieve revelation. The substitution of the imagination for thought (symbolized by the loosing of the thought-woven sails) is not enough for this exalted quest. The quest ends in death, and the immortal throbbing of the imagination continues, not yet fully alive, but never dead. The stasis of the ship, waiting on the "dim grey sea," is, as in "Fergus and the Druid," the obstacle impeding the imaginative quest. As in that poem, physical action is not the path to vision: and as vision commences, action ceases.

"The Rose of Battle" may be read as a parable of the "Rose" and the poetic quest. The intersection of the horizontal and vertical paths creates a cross (the Rood of Time), at the top of which rests the sought-after rose:

> Rose of all Roses, Rose of all the World!
> You, too, have come where the dim tides are hurled
> Upon the wharves of sorrow, and heard ring
> The bell that calls us on; the sweet far thing.

Guarding the rose are stars (as in "The Poet Pleads with the Elemental Powers"), and at the bottom of the tree-ladder, being beckoned by the imagination (the bell-buoys) but unable to ascend, are the questers (the ships), caught in time (the sea itself) and finally destroyed—eager but unable to ascend the ladder. Imagination alone is *not enough*, and the poet's problem is to discover a mode of action that lends access to this magical realm, that reconciles insight with action, knowledge with power. (Later Yeats's fine sonnet "Leda and the Swan" will pose the question: "Did she put on his knowledge with his power / Before the indifferent beak could let her drop?")

What progress has Yeats made toward reconciliation in the poems of THE ROSE? There have been many indications of *poetic* progress: more precise description, especially sharper attention to and more successful rendering of gesture; increased dramatic tension through direct confrontation, dialogue, and other means; fresh insights; a new complexity of symbol; a more vigorous commitment as opposed to the earlier brooding; and a quest for eternal beauty through Irish folklore and the ephemera of everyday life. All of this is evidence of the rapid approach of artistic maturity and even greatness. But the larger quest for reconciliation must offer much more than this; it must end in the resolution of the persistent, warring antinomies.

The dominant "idea" of THE ROSE is the conviction—expressed in the opening poem—that beauty is one identifiable eternal quality in a world of flux and death, and that this beauty can be discovered in what is passing, as well as in what has passed. Again and again the individual poems examine "eternal beauty" in its various guises—the physical loveliness of a woman (Maud Gonne, Helen of Troy, Deirdre), mystical wisdom (Fergus), human love, and others—and this quality, in all its guises, is a consolation worthy of the poet's lasting commitment. There is ample evidence in THE ROSE poems that Yeats has found beauty (and the means to transmit it) in ancient myths and everyday life; but this is a trivial discovery indeed when we remind ourselves that Yeats seeks something far more immense than the term *eternal beauty* implies: he seeks a universal harmony which will reconcile the various antinomies which clash with mounting violence in his verse from beginning to end of his career. *Eternal beauty* seems somehow too trivial a synonym for the harmony he seeks, and it is little wonder that so many critics have accused him of seeking mere prettiness (though he is innocent of the charge) in view of his use of this limiting phrase. But THE ROSE poems make it clear that the poet seeks "eternal beauty" as a means of achieving just such a harmony—an orderly reconciliation of ideal and real, of imagination and action, of eternal and ephemeral. As David Daiches points out, Yeats's purpose in writing THE ROSE is the same as his purpose in composing the prose sketches of *The Celtic Twilight*—to create an *ordered* visionary world of his own out of Irish material old and new.[16]

Yeats wrote in the introduction to that volume: "I have desired, like every artist, to create a little world out of the beautiful, plea-

16 Daiches, "W. B. Yeats—I," 118.

sant, significant things of this marred and clumsy world, and to show in a vision something of the face of Ireland to any of my own people who would look where I bid them."[17]

The problem of THE ROSE is that action, at least the kind of action the poet understands at this stage of his poetic career, is inadequate to this exalted purpose; and imagination unaided by action—though more nearly adequate—also falls short of the requirement.

In "The Man who Dreamed of Faeryland" the demands of imagination and action are more nearly equalized than in any other of THE ROSE poems. The dreamer is held in thrall by his own imagination, despite his preference for the world of commerce and everyday reality. (In this respect he is unlike the CROSSWAYS characters who sought release from reality through imagination.) As the man travels through his allotted lifetime, engrossed in his mundane world, the higher world of dream does not relinquish its hold upon him—not even in death, for "The man has found no comfort in the grave." *No comfort*—a curious phrase indeed from a young poet whose comfort has been sought *in* imagination and not apart from it; but the poem is apparently intended to balance, to some extent at least, all those other ones in which reality is the force that will not let go and imagination is the promised land. Imagination is no less desirable here than elsewhere, of course; but we view it from the opposite shore; we perceive the intricately maintained balance of the two forces, to be schematized, in not too many years, through the elaborate cones and whirling gyres of *A Vision*.

In "Who Goes with Fergus?", which may well be the finest poem of THE ROSE, the imagination wins its most triumphant moment. Here, in a compact but richly articulated structure, we gain a vision of the imagination's triumph over all creation:

> For Fergus rules the brazen cars,
> And rules the shadows of the wood,

17 W. B. Yeats, introduction to *The Celtic Twilight* (London, 1893).

> And the white breast of the dim sea
> And all dishevelled wandering stars.

Fire, earth, water, air—all are subject to him who, like Fergus, pierces " the deep wood's woven shade" and dances "upon the level shore." But this is a triumph that Yeats has not yet earned for himself—or, as we saw in "Fergus and the Druid," for Fergus, either. He speaks here out of imaginative conviction, but his proof—as offered in the poetry—is conspicuously missing. That "sweet far thing" that beckons from the human heart has not been enough; action and imagination have not yet been reconciled. The poet must find a vigorous way to do so—action in the service of imagination—or all is stagnation and defeat.

The final key to eternal beauty and universal reconciliation, then, remains undiscovered. But the poet no longer believes, as he did at times in the 1880s, that imagination is the sole and independent means of access to this solution. He recognizes already that nothing can be left behind, nothing sacrificed; if imagination is essential, then so is action. If dream is essential, then so is reality. And this realization returns us to those unresolved but at last fully recognized antinomies which are characteristic of eternal beauty, which is both destructive and beneficial, common and mystical, human and superhuman, ephemeral and eternal, real and ideal. A surrender of the will to mere dream is not adequate. The final poem of the volume once again demonstrates the necessity of contraries, for the poet argues that he is no less an Irishman for his mystical inquiries into "things discovered in the deep." He is, perhaps, the greater artist for seeming the lesser nationalist, for pushing well beyond questions of time and place into universal mysteries. The statement, not altogether convincing, is made dubious by its defensive tone; but in reflecting the poet's recognition of the need for the conjunction of opposites, and in addressing this need to the members of the real world, it is a happy conclusion to the volume.

3

THE WIND AMONG THE REEDS
and Apocalyptic Vision

CRITICS AS DIVERSE in their ways of reading Yeats as Louis Mac-
Neice, Harold Bloom, and Richard Ellmann have considered
THE WIND AMONG THE REEDS to be the culmination of Yeats's
early poetry.[1] In many ways their judgment is indisputable: certainly the moodiness of the earliest poems becomes more pro-
nounced in these, and the persistent dream motif is heightened
now into phantasmagoria; moreover, the patterns of language
and mood, the treatment of traditional themes and symbols become even more formalized in this volume. But thematically,
THE WIND AMONG THE REEDS is both an intensification of what
has preceded it and a cataclysmic turning aside from the steady
thematic progression of CROSSWAYS and THE ROSE. In the strictest
sense of the word, this is Yeats's most decadent poetry, for it
represents a collapse into destructive vision and a withering away

1 Louis MacNeice, *The Poetry of W. B. Yeats* (New York: Oxford University Press, 1941), 66; Harold Bloom, *Yeats* (New York: Oxford
University Press, 1970), 121; Richard Ellmann, *The Identity of Yeats*
(New York: Oxford University Press, 1964), 125. (Ellmann speaks
of stylistic culmination, as does MacNeice; Bloom describes the poetry
as a whole.)

from the firm resolution that has gone before it. Even if its poetic music is often more compelling than before, THE WIND AMONG THE REEDS sings a death-song, characterized by persistent images of dimness and pallor, by what MacNiece describes as "languid, lingering, or wavering rhythms," [2] and—most importantly—by apocalyptic visions. These poems represent Yeats at his least vigorous, in his most nearly escapist mood (though his particular brand of escapism has been widely misunderstood). They represent a spiritual sickness with which the poet himself is unable to come to terms, and from which he does not emerge until, possibly, the last poem—"The Fiddler of Dooney"—which is discussed at the end of this chapter.

Yeats's ambitious quest for secret wisdom that would help to reconcile the antinomies of reality and dream undergoes a crippling transformation in THE WIND AMONG THE REEDS. These poems contain no hope for any humanly attainable form of reconciliation. They voice a despairing conviction that no lasting peace or happiness is possible in this life; and this despair is alleviated only by Yeats's visionary anticipation of some better existence which may lie beyond the fiery apocalypse. This is essentially a poetry of vision; but the poet's ascent toward ultimate wisdom on his self-styled neo-Platonic ladder is interrupted by a shattering love experience, and he plunges hopelessly from his ladder as he envisions the approaching apocalypse. The result, as Ellmann describes it, is "the quicksands of the poetry of THE WIND AMONG THE REEDS, a poetry where one sinks down and down without finding bottom." [3]

Despite his despair at finding a solution to man's miseries— short of universal conflagration—Yeats is no less concerned in this volume with the conflict of opposites. A casual glance over

2 MacNeice, *The Poetry of W. B. Yeats*, 67.
3 Richard Ellmann, *Yeats: The Man and the Masks* (New York: Dutton, 1948), 159.

the individual poems will reveal the interplay of many kinds of opposite pairs:

> And never was piping so sad,
> And never was piping so gay.

> The silver apples of the moon,
> The golden apples of the sun.

> I am no more with life and death

> *The banners of East and West,*

> Until he found, with laughter and with tears,

> Lilies of death-pale hope, roses of passionate dream.

> Come clear of the nets of wrong and right;

Beyond these and other obvious oppositions among the images, Yeats explores thematically the terrible failure of the present world to satisfy the dimensions of his imagination's ideal world. This opposition—the familiar Yeatsian conflict of the real and the ideal—governs the mood of the entire volume. Representative of this mood is the poem "The Lover Tells of the Rose in His Heart":

> All things uncomely and broken, all things worn out and old,
> The cry of a child by the roadway, the creak of a lumbering cart,
> The heavy steps of the ploughman, splashing the wintry mould,
> Are wronging your image that blossoms a rose in the deeps of my
>   heart.

> The wrong of unshapely things is a wrong too great to be told;
> I hunger to build them anew and sit on a green knoll apart,
> With the earth and the sky and the water, remade, like a casket
>   of gold
> For my dreams of your image that blossoms a rose in the deeps of
>   my heart.

This little poem, often slighted among the more compelling bids for attention in the volume, indicates Yeats's radical failure to achieve the goal he set in the opening poem of THE ROSE: to find eternal beauty in "all poor foolish things that live a day" and to heed "common things that crave." Yeats cannot accept the petty imperfections which constitute almost the whole of earthly existence—a child's cry, a splash of mud, a creaking cart—because they violate his private vision of perfection. Ironically, such images have served other poets as the very essence of poetry; more ironically, they serve Yeats's own poem even as he is complaining of them. One may see this as a deliberate instance of self-irony; or he may see it, as I do, as an accidental irony which Yeats, in his present anguished state of mind, cannot appreciate. Like Coleridge, who laments the loss of his "shaping spirit of Imagination" in a poem which demonstrates admirably the presence of that spirit,[4] Yeats is oblivious to the poetical value of what he spurns.

He says in the second stanza, "I hunger to build them anew and sit on a green knoll apart...." The poet would displace the Divine Creator and remake the world according to his own design, in order to satisfy the perfect image of his beloved; then, his work done, he would isolate himself from his own ideal creation. If one takes the poet at his word (for there is always the possibility of irony), the reader is unlikely to favor this new world of children who never cry and carts that never creak; he is more likely to prescribe for the youthful Yeats the treatment which the older Yeats would one day prescribe for himself in "The Circus Animals' Desertion":

> Those masterful images because complete
> Grew in pure mind, but out of what began?
> A mound of refuse or the sweepings of a street,
> Old kettles, old bottles, and a broken can,
> Old iron, old bones, old rags, that raving slut
> Who keeps the till. Now that my ladder's gone,
> I must lie down where all the ladders start,
> In the foul rag-and-bone shop of the heart.

4 I am referring, of course, to Coleridge's "Dejection: An Ode."

But instead of lying down in the rag-and-bone shop of the heart, Yeats at this time pins his hopes for deliverance upon two outside powers: visionary revelation and the apocalypse. Of these two, vision will prove an essential source for Yeats's ultimate reconciliation of opposites, though the kind of vision which he seeks now, which comes in dream from a source beyond the self,[5] must be replaced by *inward* vision before much progress toward reconciliation can be made. Yeats was to distinguish between these two kinds of vision in 1914, at the end of RESPONSIBILITIES: alluding to the mystical wind among the reeds, he speaks of that "reed-throated whisperer" who now comes to him "inwardly" rather than as "A clear articulation in the air." As for the apocalypse—despite the rich profusion of images which it lends to these poems and the urgency with which Yeats anticipates its righting the existing wrongs of creation—its interest for Yeats seemed to dissipate rapidly after the publication of this volume, despite occasional references to it in later work.

Because Yeats does not yet seek visionary revelation from his own inner resources at this stage, and because he scorns the imperfectly created world of flesh-and-blood realities, the world he evokes in THE WIND AMONG THE REEDS is narrowly circumscribed. As a result many of the poems have the abstracted qualities of dream or nightmare: a hazy indefiniteness of action, an element of unspecified terror, phantasmagoric imagery, spatial disorientation, and a peculiarly anonymous series of characters who are not so much seen as remembered.

Contributing to this air of anonymity is Yeats's extensive and

5 Yeats explains in a note accompanying *The Wind Among the Reeds*: "I had sometimes when awake, but more often in sleep, moments of vision, a state very unlike dreaming, when these images took upon themselves what seemed an independent life and became a part of a mystic language, which seemed always as if it would bring me some strange revelation." This note was written in 1908 for the Stratford-on-Avon edition of Yeats's collected poetry and prose, as quoted in Peter Allt and Russell K. Alspach (eds.), *The Variorum Edition of the Poems of W. B. Yeats* (New York: Macmillan, 1968), 800.

erratic borrowing of esoteric imagery from his occult Golden Dawn researches, especially in descriptions of the apocalypse. But also in love poems, such as "He Mourns for the Change . . . ," esoteric images displace clarity, as if the poet were being deliberately obscure. The inherent fascination of such bizarre images as the hound with one red ear and the boar without bristles lends an element of excitement to poems in which clear identification of symbols and even images is not possible without footnotes. Why, for example, has the hound one red ear? And why is a boar without bristles going to destroy the world? We hasten to the footnotes hoping for explanation, and we come away sensing vaguely that there is a precedent for such images in the traditions of esoteric magic or in Irish folklore; but the poems remain essentially blurred.

Action, too, is often indistinct. Some poems offer only frequent, vivid flashes of fragmentary action—a toss of hair, a horse's hoof "heavy with tumult"—and the reader senses that more is happening than is being revealed. Strange, unprecedented events are hinted at, but they are confined within the speaker's or the poet's tormented imagination.

Ellmann describes the way Yeats defines the recurrent figure of the beloved lady: "Pallor, dimness, and whiteness, one lifted hand, an abundance of hair, and an indistinct bosom give her the generalized look of a Burne-Jones figure. The reiteration of the word *dream* assists in making her seem some immemorial archetype." [6] The abstraction of character, action, and image costs Yeats a good deal. For one thing, it is not easy for the reader to care about an "immemorial archetype" as he would care about a real, individualized woman. The stylization of experience distills away any sense of immediacy. The imperfections which Yeats rejects in "The Lover Tells of the Rose in His Heart"— the crying child, the creaking cart, and the mud-splashing steps

6 Ellmann, *The Identity of Yeats*, 23.

of the ploughman—seem at once more true to human experience and more useful to the poet than such images as the "cloud-pale eyelids" and "dream-dimmed eyes" of an anonymous beauty. Perhaps Ellmann is right in seeing in the anonymity of the poems an effort to make them universal: "To chill his emotions he found it convenient to make them somewhat mysterious, to set them in formal patterns, to couch them in a 'symbolic language' with many links to tradition, transforming an individual mood into one which generations of men had experienced, and to embody them in slow rhythms disengaged from the excitement of immediate experience." [7]

In setting out to achieve this effect, Yeats devises—again according to Ellmann—"the distilled self, archetypal and not personal." [8] This well describes the persona of these poems: neither Yeats nor his mask, but an impersonal distillation of himself. By abstracting not only experience but also himself, Yeats subordinates his characters and events to the one principle that activates this volume: the urgency of emotion. Even the unhappy love experience that is so frequently alluded to remains so vague that at the end one knows little more about it than that it was unhappy; but what one does perceive is the rich orchestration of *mood*. William York Tindall sees each of these poems as the embodiment of a particular mood: "Through the swooning, luscious diction, the musical, individual rhythms, the harmonies and overtones, and the interaction of many traditional but mysterious images each poem becomes the symbol of an unstated idea or mood." [9] An *unstated* idea or mood: this, too, suggests a certain degree of anonymity, as if even the moods are somehow kept under wraps. The evocation of mood at the expense of character, action, and concrete imagery is likely to produce a static

---

7 *Ibid.*, 124.   8 *Ibid.*, 123.
9 W. Y. Tindall, "The Symbolism of W. B. Yeats," in James Hall and Martin Steinmann (eds.), *The Permanence of Yeats* (New York: Macmillan, 1961), 245.

poetry; happily mood never replaces all three of these in any one poem, and the poetry—though not especially lively—is much less static than it might have been in view of Yeats's technique at this stage of his career. If Yeats makes few moral choices in these poems, he at least dramatizes the conflict of opposites in such a way as to show the difficulty of choosing; this interplay of opposites and the tension resulting from it are the principal elements which save the poems from being static.

The opening poem, "The Hosting of the Sidhe," demonstrates the conflict of opposites and the difficulty of choosing. It describes the beckoning cries of the Sidhe (identified by Yeats in a note as the poor people's term for the Tuatha De Danaan, the ancient gods of Ireland) [10] as they rush in the wind, luring men from "mortal dream" to some unnamed other kingdom. Despite the allure of these spirits ("And where is there hope or deed as fair?"), the most striking aspect of their appearance is the chilling element of phantasmagoria:

> *The winds awaken, the leaves whirl round,*
> *Our cheeks are pale, our hair is unbound,*
> *Our breasts are heaving, our eyes are agleam,*
> *Our arms are waving, our lips are apart;*
> *And if any gaze on our rushing band,*
> *We come between him and the deed of his hand,*
> *We come between him and the hope of his heart.*

Often in earlier poems the lure of the imagination seemed altogether appealing, and the poet had to remind himself, often with seeming reluctance, that it was also perilous, as in "Fergus and the Druid" and "The Rose of Battle." In this case Yeats seems more fully conscious of the painful ambivalence of the imagination, operating in response to a beauty that is as threatening to the human creature as it is alluring.

In view of the variant interpretations of the poem, it seems

10 W. B. Yeats, note accompanying "The Hosting of the Sidhe," Allt and Alspach (eds.), *The Variorum Edition*, 800.

appropriate to explain my equating the Sidhe with the lure of the imagination. One clue is the unexplained appearance of Caoilte and Niamh among the Sidhe: Caoilte is the old poet, the acquaintance of Fionn and Oisin, and Niamh is the lovely seductress who lured Oisin from his king's battles to the dreamlike pleasures of Tir-na'n Og. Members of the Fenian cycle of Irish myth, they are not members of the Tuatha De Danaan. Bloom, recalling that Caoilte is a warrior and Niamh a beauty, suggests that Yeats is making the point that the courage and splendor of the world have been taken up into the faery host.[11] But perhaps their significance is slightly more complex than this. As poet and beautiful enchantress, they are likely agents of the higher world of imagination and vision. The name "Niamh" means in Gaelic "brightness and beauty." [12] And Yeats explains in a note that Caoilte ("tossing his burning hair") once appeared to a king as a flaming man and announced that he was his "candlestick," intended to lead him on through the darkness.[13] These facts reinforce the suitability of the pair as symbols for the lure of the imagination.

Other names in the poem carry additional associations with allurement and destruction. The host of the Sidhe proceed from Knocknarea over the grave of Clooth-na-Bare. Knocknarea, an actual mountain in Sligo, is also, as Yeats himself explains, the legendary site of the deep mountaintop lake in which Maeve, weary of her faery existence, sought to drown herself.[14] Clooth-na-Bare is Gaelic for "the old woman Bare" (or, of Bare) who, the poet explains, appears in many legends as an enchantress. Her principal duty seems to have been to beckon men to the lake she inhabited and then, like the sirens of Homer, to drown them therein.[15]

11 Bloom, *Yeats*, 124.
12 M. L. Rosenthal (ed.), *Selected Poems and Two Plays of William Butler Yeats* (New York: Macmillan, 1962), 227.
13 W. B. Yeats, note accompanying "The Hosting of the Sidhe," Allt and Alspach (eds.), *The Variorum Edition*, 801.
14 *Ibid.*   15 *Ibid.*, 802.

As if such hints of their darker side were not enough, the faery hosts promise to interpose themselves between any man who gazes upon them and all his mortal hopes and deeds. Thus, distracting man from both action and hope, they offer an escape from reality. But the point is that this escape is a *punishment* for those who look upon the Sidhe, certainly not a reward. *"Empty your heart of its mortal dream,"* Niamh calls; if one obeys, he will be left, perhaps, with an empty heart.

Despite these many indications of the negative aspects of the lure of the imagination, Yeats does not resolve the poem. He confronts us with both the positive and negative values of this particular kind of enchantment, but he makes no choice. The poem ends in suspension, which is characteristic of the poems that follow, reflecting the poet's own tantalizing uncertainty as the antinomies which have occupied him from his earliest work threaten to merge into some paradoxical but as yet indistinguishable single pattern.

As in "The Hosting of the Sidhe," much attention is devoted to escape and death in other poems from THE WIND AMONG THE REEDS. There is a persistent alternation between themes of disappointed love and visions of some terrible destruction that may usher in a better world. But beyond the disappointment and destruction, beyond the slow, lingering rhythms and the images of pallor and dimness, there is another theme that makes these poems decadent: a suicide motif that winds through the volume with varying degrees of prominence, a motif so persistent that it constitutes a major theme. Escape and death are simultaneously sought after and resisted; and the forces of the poetic imagination sometimes offer a promise of remaking the fallen world, ridding it of "All things uncomely and broken, all things worn out and old," but at other times these forces seem no other than death itself. This terrible confusion is itself a theme in these poems, suggesting that Yeats's earlier efforts to order his universe have been overthrown and all is chaos. Remarkably, in the midst of

such confusion and disorder, Yeats managed to write in THE
WIND AMONG THE REEDS some of the finest individual poems of
his early period.

Critics have made much of the personal experiences which
underlie the agony expressed in this volume of poetry: Yeats's
temporary halt in entreating Maud Gonne to marry him, and his
slowly developing, guilt-ridden love affair with Mrs. Olivia
Shakespear, an affair that was not consummated—we are perhaps too dutifully informed—until Yeats's friends and hers convinced them that it ought to be.[16] Whatever his reasons may have
been—the misery of loving one woman and being unable to forget another; the grim, apocalyptic predictions of soothsayers as
the nineteenth century drew to an end; the promptings of his
own visions; or the bleaker elements of his occult studies—Yeats
was, in 1899, somewhat more than half in love with easeful death.
Having acknowledged the ambivalent summons of the imagination in the opening poem, he seems to toss out the complex issue
he has raised in that poem by summoning Armageddon in the
next one, "The Everlasting Voices":

> O sweet everlasting Voices, be still;
> Go to the guards of the heavenly fold
> And bid them wander obeying your will,
> Flame under flame, till Time be no more;
> Have you not heard that our hearts are old. . . ?

Whatever it may be that the Voices whisper of, whether perfect
beauty, an idyllic island retreat, or simply death, the Voices only
tantalize their world-weary listeners, who urge them to cease
whispering in order to proceed with the universal conflagration.

This, surely, is the most radical of all Yeats's attempts to
achieve universal harmony. I must add that from my own viewpoint it is also the least satisfying for it seems to me that Yeats
does not quite manage to bridge the enormous disparity between

16 Ellmann, *Yeats: The Man and the Masks*, 157.

the personal, immediate theme of disappointed love and the impersonal, universal theme of apocalyptic ruin. Many of these poems are perilously liable to be reduced to the thematic absurdity: "The poet's lover is cold, so he orders the end of the world." Sheer artistry enables Yeats to skim past this problem in many of the poems, and in others the problem is not resolved. Miserable in love, he welcomes the end; but the end would come, one presumes, even if he were less miserable, and this fact somewhat mitigates the charge of pettiness.

If only one could believe that Yeats's longing for apocalypse were inspired by a more comprehensive dissatisfaction with the present world, there would perhaps be no question of pettiness. But even though such phrases as the one quoted above, "our hearts are old," may imply that Yeats had more to lament than private romantic wounds, the connection between personal love and the apocalypse is a very close one throughout this volume, so close, in fact, that Yeats appears to be generalizing on the basis of this one private crisis when he concludes that devastation is the only solution. Yeats's complaint that "hearts are old" is one that he continued to make from young manhood well into his old age, and he usually supplies ample evidence of that lamentable condition. In this volume, however, only one poem, "The Song of the Old Mother," gives a reason, other than the pain of love, for the poet's despair, the reason in this case being old age. Compare Yeats's narrow brand of *weltschmerz* with that of Keats in his "Ode to a Nightingale," for example:

> Fade far away, dissolve, and quite forget
> What thou among the leaves hast never known,
> The weariness, the fever, and the fret
> Here, where men sit and hear each other groan;
> Where palsy shakes a few, sad, last grey hairs,
> Where youth grows pale, and specter-thin, and dies;
> Where but to think is to be full of sorrow
> And leaden-eyed despairs,

> Where Beauty cannot keep her lustrous eyes,
> Or new Love pine at them beyond tomorrow.

Here one senses a sorrow that rises out of *observed* suffering as well as *felt* suffering; in these poems Yeats seems as yet incapable of that larger view.

Everywhere the apocalypse is associated with personal love. The restriction in the association is evident in the title of one of the first apocalyptic poems: "He Mourns for the Change That Has Come upon Him and His Beloved, and Longs for the End of the World." That the title was originally "The Desire of Man and of Woman" and then "Mongan Laments the Change . . ." does not alter this association, since the theme is personal love, whether that of the poet himself or of a mythological persona.

Universal ruin is not the final outcome of the apocalypse as Yeats envisages it; there is a persistent suggestion that the world will be rebuilt to some higher plan, a plan more suitable for love and beauty than the present world. For all its persistence, however, this suggestion gains little concrete support. Fragmentary clues concerning the aftermath of apocalypse appear in various poems; but one who fits them together, in the manner of a jigsaw puzzle, must finally survey the result with uncertainty, for Yeats is never strictly faithful to any one symbol and is likely to shift the symbolic meaning of an image from one poem to the next, or even within a single poem. For example, the apocalyptic poems suggest that the forces of destruction will move across the world in fire; but it is unsafe to assume that any mention of "fire" in these poems is an allusion to the apocalypse, for the image has various contradictory meanings. In "He Tells of the Perfect Beauty" time is burned away ("until God burn time"), but in "A Poet to His Beloved" time itself is fire ("the pale fire of time"). And though fire is equated with death in many of the poems, in "The Song of the Old Mother" it becomes a symbol of life, which must be coaxed and tended as it grows older and dim-

mer. Elsewhere fire is passion (as in "He Gives His Beloved
Certain Rhymes"—"all men's hearts must burn and beat") or a
state of mind (as in "The Song of Wandering Aengus"—"a fire
was in my head"). The point is that one must be wary of the
temptation to assume that the apocalyptic poems are complementary in their imagery; nor may one assume that a detail in
one such poem may explain a vagueness in another.

"He Remembers Forgotten Beauty," which begins as an extravagant compliment to a lady's beauty, ends in a solemn prophecy of the apocalypse. More important, the ending suggests
that the apocalypse will come at the bidding of Beauty itself,
that the destruction of this world is to be achieved by servants of
this high power:

> I hear white Beauty sighing, too,
> For hours when all must fade like dew,
> But flame on flame, and deep on deep,
> Throne over throne where in half sleep,
> Their swords upon their iron knees,
> Brood her high lonely mysteries.

The context of the poem suggests that Beauty sighs, not because
the hour of destruction must someday come, but rather because
it has not yet come. Despite her sighing, her "mysteries" brood
with swords upon their knees, not yet ready to move, flame upon
flame, across creation. The poem does not promise that Beauty's
servants will rebuild the universe; conceivably Beauty prefers
nothingness to a world of mere ugliness. But it seems more likely
that Beauty, being a benevolent power sympathetic to the poet
and the lover, will establish a new kingdom which will benefit both
of them.

The suggestion that the fires of the apocalypse are but a necessary prelude to a higher state of being remains an elusive hint
here as elsewhere, but it gains some force in two references to
a door of fire: in "The Valley of the Black Pig"—"Master of the
still stars and of the flaming door," and in "The Travail of

Passion"—"the flaming lute-thronged angelic door is wide."
These fiery doors suggest a necessary passageway on the path to
another, timeless existence. Another clue that may suggest what
lies beyond the apocalypse is Yeats's repeated reference to the
apocalypse in certain minor poems as a stopping point in time-
duration. For example, in the poem "He Tells of a Valley Full
of Lovers" the speaker describes a dream in which he sees his
lost love approaching out of a forest, and he warns other women
present to shield their men's eyes against his lady's beauty, "*Or
remembering hers they will find no other face fair / Till all the
valleys of the world have been withered away.*" On the surface
the poem seems to be no more than a courtly compliment to a
lady's splendid beauty, like various others in the volume; but the
last line seems inappropriately grim in such an innocent context,
functioning somewhat like a memento mori. The grimness is deliberate. The word *withered* is a reminder that this lady's beauty
must waste away as must everything that is subject to time. On
the other hand, instead of reading the closing lines to mean that
the men will never again find another woman fair, one may read
them to mean that the men will find faces as fair as this one, once
the world has been withered away—that is, after the apocalypse.
The emphatic grimness of the final line, seemingly inappropriate,
invites the reader to seek a level of meaning other than the obvious one.

It is possible, I believe, to read "He Hears the Cry of the Sedge"
in this same way: until the end of time, the lover cannot lie beside
his beloved in sleep. But *after* that terrible event, which will come,
we must remember, in the service of Beauty herself, he may be
reunited with her eternally. (Still another, almost identical example may be found in "He Thinks of His Past Greatness. . . .")

It is worth noting, too, that although this particular poem's
apocalyptic imagery is almost entirely destructive, a single image
emerges to suggest the possibility of a positive result beyond the
universal fire:

> *Until the axle break*
> *That keeps the stars in their round,*
> *And hands hurl in the deep*
> *The banners of East and West*

The axle breaks of itself, suggesting a collapse of universal machinery that plunges all creation into chaos; but there are *hands*
which hurl the banners of East and West into the deep, suggesting
a guiding principle behind the destruction, one that must be pre-
sumed to outlive that terrible hour.

One of the first apocalyptic poems bears the curious title, "He
Bids His Beloved Be at Peace"; what lover indeed is likely to be
"at peace" during the hour of apocalypse? But here, too, Yeats
may be suggesting that the lovers must endure the apocalypse as
a necessary prelude to eternal joy. As "the Horses of Disaster
plunge in the heavy clay," the speaker says to his lady:

> Beloved, let your eyes half close, and your heart beat
> Over my heart, and your hair fall over my breast,
> Drowning love's lonely hour in deep twilight of rest,
> And hiding their tossing manes and their tumultuous feet.

Yeats seems to propose personal love as a shield against eternal
ruin, just as the lady's hair is to shield her lover from the sight
of the Horses of Disaster.

Perhaps the best known and finest of the apocalyptic poems in
THE WIND AMONG THE REEDS is "The Secret Rose," which makes
more explicit both the idea that the apocalypse will come at
Beauty's bidding and the expectation of a new and better world
beyond that event. The speaker calls upon the Rose (which seems
to be Eternal Beauty, as in the previous volume of poems) and
asks to be enfolded in the deep sleep of Beauty along with the
ancient heroes:

> . . . I, too, await
> The hour of thy great wind of love and hate.
> When shall the stars be blown about the sky,
> Like the sparks blown out of a smithy, and die?

> Surely thine hour has come, thy great wind blows,
> Far-off, most secret, and inviolate Rose?

The image of stars being blown about the sky like sparks from a smithy, besides serving as a powerful visual impression of the apocalypse, suggests that the worldly destruction is but a by-product of a *creative* process rather than a merely destructive one.

Some observers, like Bloom, sense an ambivalence in Yeats's summoning the apocalypse in this poem: "Yeats wants and does not want the great wind to rise. . . . The Rose is best kept far-off, most secret, and inviolate, for if the hour of hours gives at last the sought love and creation, it must give also unsought hate and destruction, the end of nature and of human nature."[17] Although I feel that such an ambivalence would enrich this particular poem as it does so many others, I cannot find much support in the poem for Bloom's reading. The whole poem expresses a longing to join such men as the Magi, Cuchulain, and Fergus in Beauty's province "beyond the stir / And tumult of defeated dreams," with no apparent reluctance at all. Certainly it is noteworthy that the great destructive wind of Beauty is called "thy great wind of love and hate," but Bloom may burden this line with too much significance in suggesting that it is evidence of ambivalence; it seems more likely to me, in view of the mood of urgent longing throughout the poem, that the line suggests reconciliation of the "love and hate" opposites through the act of universal destruction which will end in perfect peace and beauty. Another possibility is that Yeats here refers to Beauty's love of perfection and hate of imperfection—the motive behind apocalypse.

Nor do I agree that Yeats feels that the Rose "is best kept far-off, most secret, and inviolate." After all, he is *summoning* the Rose, which is not the same as holding it at arm's length. It is

17 Bloom, *Yeats*, 132.

inviolate because it is Eternal Beauty as opposed to temporal beauty, which is always violated by time in the fallen world of creation. Yeats seems to draw comfort from its inviolability; he does not even consider the possibility of Ideal or Eternal Beauty's being sullied, let alone conclude that it is "best kept" inviolate.

Nevertheless, I would like to agree with Bloom's reading even though I cannot. If Yeats did express ambivalent feelings about the apocalypse he so persistently beckons toward in these poems, his position would seem more sympathetic and more responsible. But without that ambivalence his calling up the apocalypse is an act of despair, no more and no less; for even if he foresees some better world beyond the apocalypse, he is nevertheless abandoning all faith in the heart's "foul rag-and-bone shop," the entire created world. In rejecting transient, earthly beauty because it is transient and all earthly things because they are imperfect, Yeats has fallen as far away as he was ever to fall from the ambitious determination to reconcile the real and the ideal by unifying them. Here, instead of unifying he would simply replace one with the other. Elsewhere his imaginative efforts toward reconciliation return always to *this* world, for elsewhere he would not forsake the precious if often painful realities of mortal life or his dream of a timeless and flawless other world.

So much, then, for the theme of apocalyptic reconciliation—or, more properly, apocalyptic replacement of the real by the ideal. There is one poem in the volume, a short and not especially good one, which suggests another form of reconciliation, the perfection of human love—specifically, sexual love. Since I have said that the volume contains no hope for any humanly attainable form of reconciliation, I would like to account for this one. Called "The Heart of the Woman," it presents a woman's defense of her decision to abandon her parents' home, "brimmed up with prayer and rest," in order to elope with her lover. The poem ends:

> The shadowy blossom of my hair
> Will hide us from the bitter storm.

> O hiding hair and dewy eyes,
> I am no more with life and death,
> My heart upon his warm heart lies,
> My breath is mixed into his breath.

Physically united with her lover, she is heedless of earthly comforts and imagines that she has escaped the hold of both life and death. The line "I am no more with life and death" suggests a perfect balancing of the antinomies, a reconciliation that is complete for these two fortunate mortals even if it does not embrace the whole world. It is possible, perhaps, to read this poem as Yeats's envious view of fulfillment in love as opposed to his own romantic frustration; doubtless he *is* envious of these lovers, but more likely he is commenting upon the woman's naivete rather than sharing her confidence that she has transcended all earthly cares. The antinomies only *seem* balanced; for the lovers, caught in the inescapable march of time, must change, and so must their love change. Her boast that her shadowy hair will hide her and her lover from the "bitter storm" (reality or possibly the apocalypse) seems specious indeed, though several other poems in the volume express this same confidence in the protective power of a woman's hair (Tindall discusses this motif as the "hair-tent").[18] Admittedly, nothing in the poem hints that the march of time will affect the lovers; but the poem immediately preceding this one, "The Song of the Old Mother," and an earlier one, "The Unappeasable Host," may have some bearing upon this one, just as in CROSSWAYS one poem tempers or even contradicts the assertions of another.

In "The Unappeasable Host" a mother kisses her wailing child (that "imperfection" that Yeats wishes to eradicate in the world to come) as she hears the desolate winds that lure her to her grave. Though she recognizes the "Danaan children" (*i.e.*, the Sidhe) in the cry of the wind, she is irresistibly attracted: "O heart the

18 John Unterecker also discusses this image in *A Reader's Guide to William Butler Yeats* (New York: Noonday Press, 1959), 92.

winds have shaken, the unappeasable host / Is comelier than candles at Mother Mary's feet." Yeats explains his use of the wind in these poems thus: "I use the wind as a symbol of vague desires and hopes . . . wind and spirit and vague desire have been associated everywhere."[19] If this is so, the desolate winds that whisper of death to the young mother are simply reflections of her own vague desires.

"The Song of the Old Mother" complements this one with its thoroughly negative image of old age. Whereas the young may lie idle and dream, the old mother must work hard even though her spark of life, symbolically the "seed of the fire," becomes "feeble and cold." By arranging these three poems so that one sees the young mother and the old mother before encountering the young lover who has just eloped, Yeats invites the reader to perceive the fate that awaits this naive young woman as she grows older. Moreover, immediately following the poem about the young woman is a pair of poems about love gone sour: "The Lover Mourns for the Loss of Love" and "He Mourns for the Change That Has Come Upon Him and His Beloved. . . ." These, too, suggest that "the old despair" is likely to return.

The final poem in THE WIND AMONG THE REEDS is the relatively lighthearted "The Fiddler of Dooney," which was written somewhat earlier than most of the other poems in the volume, and at first reading seems to have little relation to those preceding it. The bleak moodiness, the despair, the apocalyptic visions are all absent from this simple, straightforward little poem in which the fiddler of Dooney boasts of his musical excellence. But a closer look reveals that it is, after all, related to the others, principally in its looking forward, though in a markedly different frame of mind, to the day of judgment:

19 W. B. Yeats, note accompanying "Michael Robartes asks Forgiveness because of his Many Moods," Allt and Alspach (eds.), *The Variorum Edition,* 806.

> When we come at the end of time
> To Peter sitting in state,
> He will smile on the three old spirits,
> But call me first through the gate;
>
> For the good are always the merry,
> Save by an evil chance,
> And the merry love the fiddle,
> And the merry love to dance.

Always devoted to the wisdom of simple folk, Yeats uses this lively poem as an antidote to the spiritual sickness that pervades this volume of poetry. Its energy, simplicity, and optimistic good faith represent a return to *terra firma* after the bottomless, anguished spiritual drifting of the majority of the other poems. The good are always merry, the fiddler tells us, "Save by an evil chance." Perhaps it was but an "evil chance" that cost the lover of these poems his terrible disappointment with his lost lady, and perhaps—as the inclusion and placement of the poem suggest—there is a strong chance of recovery from this protracted melancholia after all. The volume ends with the delightful image of the blessed in heaven dancing to the fiddler's joyous music "like a wave of the sea." The sea is one of Yeats's favorite symbols for the life force. A volume that began with an errie ride over a grave ("The Hosting of the Sidhe") thus ends on the vastly more positive note of a dance like the sea.

"Every writer," Yeats comments in an essay on Synge, "even every small writer, who has belonged to the great tradition, has had his dream of an impossibly noble life, and the greater he is, the more does it seem to plunge him into some beautiful or bitter reverie."[20] If the beauty and bitterness of Yeats's own reveries in THE WIND AMONG THE REEDS are an indication of his great-

---

20 W. B. Yeats, preface to *The Well of the Saints* by John Millington Synge (1905), in Yeats, *Essays and Introductions* (New York: Macmillan, 1961), 303.

ness, then he was already very great indeed. His anguished yearning for the apocalypse dominates the volume, though happily the final poem suggests that the eye of the storm is past and recovery is imminent. As F. R. Leavis observes, though the volume is "a poetry of withdrawal," it is astonishingly vital; "to nurse a luxury of defeat was not in Mr. Yeats's character; he was too strong and alive."[21]

In his ambitious book-length study of this volume Allen R. Grossman sees THE WIND AMONG THE REEDS as a far more positive step in Yeats's career than I do. Instead of a document of despairing moodiness, relieved only by a distant hope of purgation through apocalypse, Grossman sees it as "the search for poetic knowledge" which defines itself as "an account of personal origins."[22] Although it would be convenient for me to read the apocalypse as a symbol for imagination itself in this study, I am unable to share Grossman's conviction, which is nonetheless a thought-provoking one: "The means of the destruction of time was poetry, which had behind it all the power of the unsatisfied libido. The Black Pig was Yeats' symbol of the imagination which brought the last judgment upon the world by destroying it in its material and accidental mode in order that it might be recreated ideal, essential, and fulfilling."[23]

At any rate, even if Yeats's prophecy of the apocalypse lingers in it, the final poem predicts a new strength and vitality. The next volume of poems, which takes us into the new century, will reveal the extent of this anticipated recovery.

21 F. R. Leavis, selection from *New Bearings in English Poetry* (London, 1932), in Hall and Steinmann (eds.), *The Permanence of Yeats*, 152.
22 Allen R. Grossman, *Poetic Knowledge in the Early Yeats: A Study of "The Wind Among the Reeds"* (Charlottesville: University Press of Virginia, 1969), xiv.
23 *Ibid.*, 27.

4

A New Voice
for the Old Bitterness,
1904–1910

IN THE SEVEN WOODS (1904) and FROM 'THE GREEN HELMET
AND OTHER POEMS' (1910) are generally considered to mark the
beginning of Yeats's middle period, during which he forsook the
romantic melancholia, dense imagery, and comparatively tor-
tured syntax of his early period in favor of a simpler, more direct
style, sparse, uncluttered, and closer to the realities of his particular time and place. Certainly there is no disputing these general
distinctions between the two periods, for the reader who proceeds
directly into IN THE SEVEN WOODS after completing THE WIND
AMONG THE REEDS cannot fail to be struck by the abrupt and
wholesale shifts in style, theme, and imagery. It is rather like
reading the poetry of a man who has been dangerously ill for a
long time and whose fever has just broken. The disappointing
aspect of this volume, however, is that a man who in his illness
suffers apocalyptic visions and extreme spiritual anguish is likely
to be considerably more interesting to the lover of poetry than the
man who is calmly recuperative. I find no company other than
Harold Bloom in my conviction that these "middle period" poems

fall short of the power of those of the early period.[1] With the
turbulence of Yeats's early verse went his inspiration, and IN THE
SEVEN WOODS seems—on the whole—a group of poems largely
uninspired. There are good moments and bad in almost all the
poems (though one wonders if Yeats ever wrote worse than "O
Do Not Love Too Long"), but only a handful are worthy to be
placed alongside his best work: "Adam's Curse," the obvious
choice among all of them; probably "The Folly of Being Comforted"; and possibly "The Players Ask for a Blessing on the
Psalteries and on Themselves."

Although the possible reasons for this disappointing presentation are beyond the scope of this discussion, it seems worth noting
Bloom's suggestion that Yeats was "appalled by the personal
wreck of his own Romanticism" and attempted at this stage of
his career to become "an anti-Romantic revisionist of English
poetry," a pose that went against his grain.[2] A simpler answer
may be that his deliberate adoption of a new poetic technique
posed problems of accommodation which only much practice
could solve. At any rate, before discussing the poems themselves,
it is only fair to acknowledge a personal bias in favor of Bloom's
opinion that—as he rather testily puts it—"one is free to think
that the movement between the two volumes is an improvement
in attitude, but one is deficient in taste and judgment to think
the movement an aesthetic advance."[3]

As Yeats gains his moorings with his new technique, he gives
the theme of reconciliation of opposites a rather static treatment.
Though the poems demonstrate his continuing struggle with the
antinomies of human experience and imply his need to reconcile
them, the battle seems to have reached a temporary stalemate.
Old themes repeat themselves without much innovation except
in style, and perhaps this is one reason for the apparent stale-

1 Harold Bloom, *Yeats* (New York: Oxford University Press, 1970),
161.
2 *Ibid.*, 162–63.   3 *Ibid.*, 163.

mate: Yeats is preoccupied with saying the old things in the new way.

If there is scarcely any progress toward reconciliation, there is even regression in one area: the social division within Yeats's audience. Instead of advancing from a sectarian to an increasingly comprehensive view of humanity, in the manner of the neo-Platonic progressions he so much admires, Yeats suddenly becomes aware that his large audience consists of two incompatible groups—the secular masses who are insensitive to the refinements of his work and those sensitively attuned few upon whose appreciation he can rely. This discovery, no doubt largely the result of his assuming a public role in the Irish theater movement (and encountering widespread hostility there), has markedly unattractive effects upon the poetry, as I shall attempt to demonstrate in discussing the opening poem, "In the Seven Woods." My point is that instead of reconciliation and consequent unity, Yeats slips backward in the social issue, into division and disharmony.

If, employing the wisdom of hindsight, one looks from the achievement of *A Vision* to the earlier time of the SEVEN WOODS poems, he may discern the rudimentary outlines of certain motifs which would occupy the poet in his later poetry and in *A Vision*—motifs which, if not especially significant in the SEVEN WOODS poems, would eventually contribute to the poet's most comprehensive effort at universal reconciliation. For this reason alone the motifs merit careful examination. One such element is Yeats's introduction of the mask. Another is his new and ambitious use of the moon image compatible with its function in *A Vision*. A more distinct example than either of these is the often reiterated analogy between man's condition and the condition of physical nature, a step—if only a slight one—toward merging man and nature into one comprehensive pattern.

Yeats's major themes from his earlier verse remain constant in this volume, though they may be difficult to recognize in their new and sparser trappings. Disappointment in love, which was

the chief impetus behind the writing of most of THE WIND AMONG
THE REEDS, is still prominent, with the notable difference that
the lover's wounds have now begun to heal as he looks sadly
backward to the experience which caused them. The prophecies
of Armageddon, so closely associated with love's agony in the
previous volume, are here also, though Yeats only whispers of
Armageddon now in an esoteric double-talk which seems meant
for the full understanding of only a select few readers. Such
whispering to the select few is one result of the poet's new awareness of his divided audience, a result which Ellmann calls the
"secularization" of this volume.[4] Finally, the conflict between
man's desire for permanence and the relentless march of time
constitutes the most distinctive antinomial theme of this volume.

Predictably, the opening poem, which is the title poem, reveals
a great deal about those that follow. Typical of them is this poem's
intricate irony which, instead of enriching the poem as the best
Yeatsian irony does, serves to split the poem into two parallel
layers, a surface for secular consumption and an underlying level
for the initiates. The ostensible point of the poem (which, like
most of the others in this volume, offers an easily extractable
theme) is that nature has been a comfort to the forlorn speaker.
The poem begins in a straightforward manner:

> I have heard the pigeons of the Seven Woods
> Make their faint thunder, and the garden bees
> Hum in the lime-tree flowers; and put away
> The unavailing outcries and the old bitterness
> That empty the heart.

Thanks to the pigeons and bees, the speaker has been able to
renounce his bitterness. But the next lines complicate his claim
considerably by suggesting that it is spurious:

> I have forgot awhile
> Tara uprooted, and new commonness

4 Richard Ellmann, *The Identity of Yeats* (New York: Oxford University Press, 1964), 103.

Upon the throne and crying about the streets
And hanging its paper flowers from post to post,
Because it is alone of all things happy.

Obviously such an emphatic denunciation of the reign of Edward VII does not support the speaker's claim that he has forgotten its existence for awhile; in fact, he remains all too conscious of it.

The second passage has images which are neatly parallel to those in the first passenge: the bees that hum in the flowers contrast with the new commonness that cries in the streets, and the reality of lime-tree flowers contrasts with the artificiality of paper flowers hanging from the posts. These parallels establish a certain balance and order within the poem; but this balance is unsettled in two ways: by the disparity between the speaker's claiming to have lost his bitterness and the evidence that he has not done so, and by the puzzling explanation the speaker offers for having put such unpleasantness out of his mind: "Because it is alone of all things happy." The apparent antecedent for the "it" of this line is the "new commonness"; if read this way, the poem suggests that its speaker desires to have no part in such happiness; only the common, in such a fallen world, can attain it.

The final passage completes the speaker's curious distinction between himself and the new commonness:

I am contented, for I know that Quiet
Wanders laughing and eating her wild heart
Among pigeons and bees, while that Great Archer,
Who but awaits His hour to shoot, still hangs
A cloudy quiver over Pairc-na-lee.

Since the commonness is "alone of all things happy," the speaker must be *contented* rather than happy. The reason for his contentment, presumably the looming presence of Quiet and the Great Archer, is an altogether unsettling one. Quiet, wandering and laughing and eating her own heart, is a grotesque and alarming figure, completely unlike the gentle "Maid Quiet" of the previous volume, who vanished while "Nodding her russet hood." As Ellmann amusingly puts it, "Her abandoned autophagy is close to misconduct."[5] The image of the Great Archer "Who but awaits His hour to shoot" is no more likely to inspire complacency than is Quiet.

The identity of the Archer is apparently debatable. Unterecker identifies him as Sagittarius, though he offers no reason for his choice.[6] As the constellation of the archer, Sagittarius is certainly a reasonable candidate; his appropriateness is reinforced, perhaps, by the fact that the sun is in Sagittarius at the time of the winter solstice, for the image may suggest in the poem a prophecy of change, as from one season to another. But Ellmann sees more in the image, suggesting that it may represent either God, about to set off the apocalypse, or merely Jupiter Pluvius, about to release a thunder shower. "The possibility of reading it in either apocalyptic or climatic terms . . . indicates Yeats's increasing mindfulness of his predominantly secular audience."[7]

This increasing mindfulness may have put Yeats's diction on a fresher and more vigorous path, as evidenced by the abrupt movement toward simple, almost colloquial language in some of these poems; but aesthetically, it has betrayed him. The irony which splits "In the Seven Woods" into two levels of meaning does not enrich the poem, because the surface level is deceptive rather than ironical. "Nature has led me to forget ugly realities of the present," the speaker says, "and I am content to behold stillness and rainfall." In fact, the speaker has not forgotten those realities for a moment and he eagerly awaits the apocalypse which alone will be capable of correcting them. One may ask, is it possible that Yeats intends for the irony to serve at the expense of the speaker? If so, the problem of the split within the poem

5 *Ibid.*, 101.
6 John Unterecker, *A Reader's Guide to William Butler Yeats* (New York: Noonday Press, 1959), 98.
7 Ellmann, *The Identity of Yeats*, 103.

would be solved, and this speaker would be classified along with the Happy Shepherd and others as personae whose insights are more restricted than those of the poet. But the speaker of "In the Seven Woods" all too clearly resembles Yeats himself. One might also argue that the poem represents an artistic reconciliation in which the two alien components of the audience blend into one—each perceiving the same truth, but in different degrees. But this is not the case either, since the two levels of meaning are not complementary but contradictory; and their effect, consequently, is division rather than unity.

Elsewhere Yeats uses irony to support two or more levels of meaning simultaneously, with each meaning having a necessary function in the poem, contributing to its total meaning. But here it is as if Yeats were mouthing lame insincerities to an audience whom he did not respect, while his distinguished friends, waiting in the wings, delighted in the *doubles-entendres*. It is not a pretty picture of Yeats the public man, and it will become even less so.

Although one can find, if he searches carefully enough, evidence of masks in Yeats's first poems, "In the Seven Woods" marks the earliest appearance of the particular form the mask would have in the later poetry and in *A Vision*: it is not merely a disguise for the poet's own voice, but rather his antiself, the exact polar opposite of his own nature. At first the introduction of the mask in its final form may seem a sign of progress; and in a sense, of course, it is. But if the mask has assumed the form of the *Vision* mask, it has decidedly not assumed the role of the *Vision* mask as a means of attaining unity. In *A Vision*, man's pursuit of his antiself is a means of gathering unto himself a more comprehensive experience of human life. The introvert embraces the life of the extravert; the contemplative man assumes the role of the active man; and so on. Thus the mask serves as a means of reconciling opposites. Here, however, the speaker of "In the Seven Woods" seems merely to retreat beyond the barrier of his mask, addressing his secular audience as a passive, con-

tented man while his actual mood of bitterness and his actual hope
of violent destruction may be noted and understood only by the
initiated few. Hence the mask here represents not a means of
reconciliation but rather a growing consciousness of disharmony
to which the poet responds by splitting himself into two opposing
faces. Reconciliation, synthesis, and unity are clearly a long way
off.

The mask occurs in several of these poems—"Never Give All
the Heart," "The Old Men Admiring Themselves in the Water,"
and possibly "Adam's Curse," depending upon interpretation.
In the first of these the poet proclaims the superiority of what
seems over what *is*, though his tone is ironical:

> Never give all the heart, for love
> Will hardly seem worth thinking of
> To passionate women if it seem
> Certain, and they never dream
> That it fades out from kiss to kiss;
> For everything that's lovely is
> But a brief, dreamy, kind delight.
> O never give the heart outright,
> For they, for all smooth lips can say,
> Have given their hearts up to the play.
> And who could play it well enough
> If deaf and dumb and blind with love?
> He that made this knows all the cost,
> For he gave all his heart and lost.

The women surpass the embittered speaker at love because they
maintain sufficient detachment to be able to "play" their roles
well. And in their role-playing they manage a curious, artificial
reconciliation between man's desire to love forever and the sad
fact that love "fades out from kiss to kiss." If the ladies' mask
requires a deception, at least it has the dual advantage of lending
an illusion of permanence to love and of protecting them from
heartbreak. The speaker, evidently Yeats himself, has been buf-

feted by reality (real love, real passion, and the real impermanence of love) because he has failed to make a pretense, that is,
to secure himself from pain by assuming a mask. Here, as before,
true reconciliation and unity are remote indeed.

I may seem to stretch a point by including "The Old Men
Admiring Themselves in the Water" as an example of Yeats's
mask, but I believe that the poem supports such an approach.
Part of the poem's effect depends upon the irony in the title:
instead of "admiring" themselves in the water, the old men are
lamenting the ravages of time. This points up the disparity between what the men are and what they look like, and the image
they see reflected in the water is a mask. Admittedly, this one is
not the *Vision* mask of the antiself, but it does present a false
face if not necessarily an opposite self. This application of the
mask image is a counterpart to the self-imposed mask of the
poems discussed earlier, for here the mask is unavoidably imposed from outside the self. The old men's hands resemble claws,
and their knees are twisted like thorn-trees; but if their exterior
selves become more and more like mere animal or even plant
life, they are no less capable of poignantly human insight: " 'All
that's beautiful drifts away / Like the waters.' " Here, too, the
mask works *against* reconciliation and unity; time brings only
loss of beauty and insight into that irreversible loss.

"Adam's Curse" examines a corollary principle: the necessity
for deception, for pose. Women must "labour to be beautiful,"
and the poet's work, though much labored over, must "seem a
moment's thought." The products of time must seem spontaneous
and natural. And, conscious again of his secular audience, the
poet laments:

> For to articulate sweet sounds together
> Is to work harder than all these, and yet
> Be thought an idler by the noisy set
> Of bankers, schoolmasters, and clergymen
> The martyrs call the world.

Hence, in requiring of himself a work of art that is achieved only through careful artifice, he is aware that even successful art cannot win the acclaim of the busy world outside. Once again, reconciliation into a single design seems very far away.

If Yeats's divisive social consciousness and his adoption of the mask seem to remove him farther than before from his quest to reconcile the contrary forces of human life, at least his treatment of the kinship between his characters and nature suggests a certain step toward unity. Earlier, in CROSSWAYS, the characters sought in vain for a sympathetic response from nature, and there was evidence that nature held mysterious secrets which she could share if she but chose. In THE ROSE and especially in THE WIND AMONG THE REEDS, natural imagery was replaced or augmented by the supernatural. In the latter volume, in fact, the destruction of all of nature was anticipated with religious fervor, for destruction of all that is subject to time and change must precede that higher order of existence which only the poetic imagination could envisage. Now, as Yeats returns to *terra firma* and surveys the actual, physical world surrounding him, he again draws upon images from nature.

The most important of these is the moon, which interested Yeats sporadically in earlier work but gains new prominence here. One should, of course, remain carefully alert to Yeats's suns and moons at this stage, in order to trace their evolution toward symbolic culmination in the *Vision* poems. The moon image occurs in five of these poems, and most of the descriptions are so consistent that a characterization emerges from them. The moon is *pale, dim, hollow*, and *worn* by time. In only one poem, "The Ragged Wood," does the moon appear in another guise; here, instead of being fragile, worn, and empty, it is "that sliding silver-shoed / Pale silver-proud queen-woman of the sky," one of the most musical descriptions Yeats ever wrote. As for the moon's activity, it is for the most part a mere silent witness, lending atmosphere to the human activities taking place beneath it.

But once, in "The Withering of the Boughs," it speaks; and once again, in "The Happy Townland," it intervenes in the affairs of men to the extent of attempting to turn a traveler back from his journey. In "The Withering of the Boughs" the speaker seems to be entreating the moon to lend him its "merry and tender and piti-ful words," but the moon confines its voice to "murmuring to the birds." I find this especially interesting, since in this poem the moon is typically spoken of as "honey-pale" and "dim," an unlikely source for "merry" words. The suggestion, here as in the earlier CROSSWAYS poems, is that the moon harbors secrets and surprises which it is loath to divulge. Even in "The Happy Townland," when the moon plucks at the traveler's rein, its actual intention is unclear; we assume that it means to send the traveler home again, but we cannot even guess at its motive.

In the last three of the five poems in which the moon image occurs, the sun also appears. Although Yeats has obviously not yet devised the elaborate system of solar-lunar opposition which determines the form of *A Vision*'s system, he has already begun to make dramatic use of this opposition. In "Under the Moon" the "Seven old sisters [the Pleiades? or a mythological variant of the Fates?] wind the threads of the long-lived ones" in a place called Land-under-Wave, where they are "out of the moon's light and the sun's." This absence of solar or lunar light underscores their supernatural remoteness from all normal human activity. Elsewhere, in "The Ragged Wood," the speaker reflects upon what the queen-woman moon may have said "When the sun looked out of his golden hood," implying a close if obscure rela-tionship between sun and moon. "The Happy Townland" pre-sents this relationship less obscurely; the sun is "*laughing sweetly*" as the traveler proceeds toward the mysterious townland, but the moon plucks at his reins as if to turn him back. Since the town-land is "*the world's bane*," the moon's warning seems appropriate and suggests that Yeats is beginning already to ally himself with lunar rather than solar forces. If sun and moon are not yet shown to govern men's lives, they demonstrate in these few poems increasing involvement in human affairs.

Sun and moon, however, are not the only evidence of the growing relationship between man and nature in the SEVEN WOODS poems. Individuals, groups of men, and even states of mind are linked to elements of physical nature. Maud Gonne, for example, is twice associated with nature: in "The Arrow" she is "Delicate in colour as apple blossom" (Yeats having first seen her sitting before a window through which apple blossoms were visible),[8] and in "The Folly of Being Comforted" the speaker recalls a time when "all the wild summer was in her gaze." These and later associations with nature exalt this lady into a mythic figure finer and grander than any mere mortal woman. On the other hand, the old men in "The Old Men Admiring Themselves in the Water" seem diminished rather than apotheosized by their increasing relation to nature—their knees twisted like old trees and their claw-like hands.

The relationship continues even to states of mind. The cause of "The Withering of the Boughs," we learn in the poem's refrain, is not the wintry wind, as one might expect, but the fact that the speaker has told his dreams to the boughs. The would-be lovers in "Adam's Curse" are "As weary-hearted as that hollow moon." Elsewhere such analogies as courage breaking like an old tree in the wind, anger like noisy clouds, and bodies and blood like flooded waters ("Red Hanrahan's Song About Ireland"), all link man and nature in some mysterious, romantic way.

As the preceding discussion has indicated, in most of the SEVEN WOODS poems the problem of reconciliation is only implicit, though the poems do reflect Yeats's continuing quest for harmony and unity. There is but little progress toward unity in

8 William Butler Yeats, *The Autobiography of William Butler Yeats* (New York: Macmillan, 1965), 82.

these poems; the insights recorded in them involve a growing consciousness of separateness and discord. Such is true also of Yeats's persistent concern in these poems with the problem of man's yearning for permanence in the face of all-consuming time. No means of reconciliation is apparent; the poems merely express the problem with mounting urgency and apparent despair. A good example is the conclusion of "The Players Ask for a Blessing on the Psalteries and on Themselves":

> *Third Voice.* O kinsmen of the Three in One,
>   O kinsmen, bless the hands that play.
>   The notes they waken shall live on
>   When all this heavy history's done;
>   Our hands, our hands must ebb away.
>
> *Three Voices* [*together*]. The proud and careless notes
>   live on,
>   But bless our hands that ebb away.

The final poem in the volume is in many ways the most interesting, for in "The Happy Townland" Yeats toys with a number of opposing forces: nature and art, aristocrat and peasant, stability and change, reality and the ideal. To say that the poet is *toying* with these themes seems more accurate than to suggest that he is completely absorbed in them, or that he orchestrates them with the kind of structural mastery that has become synonymous with his name. It is a playful poem, though at the same time a serious one. The first stanza introduces several of its themes:

> There's many a strong farmer
> Whose heart would break in two,
> If he could see the townland
> That we are riding to;
> Boughs have their fruit and blossom
> At all times of the year;
> Rivers are running over
> With red beer and brown beer.

An old man plays the bagpipes
In a golden and silver wood;
Queens, their eyes blue like the ice,
Are dancing in a crowd.

This is the happy townland of the imagination, where the
separate kingdoms of man and nature have become confused (as
shown by the rivers overflowing with beer) and the natural order
as man has experienced it in the real world has been overthrown
(as indicated by the trees' bearing fruit and blossom year-round).
It is a land where royalty democratically step down from their
thrones and dance in the crowd. So far the townland might be the
Sunday pipe dream of an Irish peasant; but the old man playing
bagpipes in a gold and silver wood complicates the imagery and
introduces a more sophisticated symbolism. The old man suggests Pan, no longer young after so many centuries, and now playing bagpipes rather than his simple reed flute. Rather than the
simpler forest of mythology, a forest made of precious metals is
the one inhabited by this older Pan. All of this seems to represent
a higher form of art which has evolved through the ages, in one
sense superior to the less complicated ancient forms, but in another sense corresponding closely to them. Indeed, it may be fair
to account for this artificial forest as a prototype for the later
Byzantium, with its golden boughs and artificial birds.

Imagination has not simply *overthrown* nature in this utopian
idyll; rather, it has heightened the natural forms into the artificial
forms of art (bagpipes rather than reed, gold and silver wood
rather than living trees). Death itself, in this higher realm of the
imagination, has become artificial, even if the outward forms of
sword fights and dying remain the same: "But all that are killed
in battle/ Awaken to life again."

Significantly, swords lifted from the *golden* and *silver* boughs
cannot maim or kill. Like Byzantium, the "happy townland" is
superior to the natural world—or at least appears to be until one
carefully weighs the matter. The old man making music in the

happy townland reminds one, perhaps, of the old man in "Sailing to Byzantium" who, being out of place in the natural world, is but a paltry thing unless "Soul clap its hands and sing." Golden boughs occur in both poems, and Gabriel's horn of "hammered silver" corresponds to the music-making bird of Byzantium who has

> such a form as Grecian goldsmiths make
> Of hammered gold and gold enamelling
> To keep a drowsy Emperor awake;
> Or set upon a golden bough to sing
> To lords and ladies of Byzantium
> Of what is past, or passing, or to come.

But the conclusion to "Sailing to Byzantium" indicates that instead of Byzantium being superior to the natural world, the two worlds are interdependent; for the drowsy emperor and his court can only be kept awake by hearing of that other world, the world of time. So, too, in "The Happy Townland" does Yeats qualify the apparent superiority of the kingdom of the imagination, though the brilliant reconciliation of opposites which he achieves in "Sailing to Byzantium" is not yet possible. Instead, he undercuts the rosy picture of the idyllic townland with various suggestions of destruction, possibly even of the apocalypse. Six times in the stanzaic refrain the little fox describes the happy townland as "the world's bane," and the poem ends with this curious phrase. In what way can this merry town prove to be the destruction of the world? Perhaps the opening lines supply the first clue:

> There's many a strong farmer
> *Whose heart would break in two* [9]
> If he could see the townland
> That we are riding to.

The farmers' hearts are considered again at the end of the second stanza:

---

9 Italics mine.

> It is lucky that their story
> Is not known among men,
> For O, the strong farmers
> That would let the spade lie,
> Their hearts would be like a cup
> That somebody had drunk dry.

The land of perfection and ease is not compatible with the world of time and labor. No mere complement to the natural world, the townland of the imagination is a repudiation of it. Not merely an improvement over it, the townland is a not altogether desirable substitution for it.

In the final stanza Yeats simultaneously presents (a) a pastoral paradise so enchanting that the archangels themselves pause to enjoy it and (b) the apocalypse cunningly concealed beneath the surface:

> Michael will unhook his trumpet
> From a bough overhead,
> And blow a little noise
> When the supper has been spread.
> Gabriel will come from the water
> With a fish-tail, and talk
> Of wonders that have happened
> On wet roads where men walk,
> And lift up an old horn
> Of hammered silver, and drink
> Till he has fallen asleep
> Upon the starry brink.

Michael, of course, is the warrior archangel; usually depicted with sword in hand, he is the conqueror of Satan. Gabriel, the divine herald, appeared to Mary at the Annunciation and will appear again as trumpeter of the Last Judgment. In the poem these traditional roles have become somewhat confused. Whereas the townsmen have lifted their swords from the golden boughs, Michael—who might be expected to take a sword—takes a trumpet instead. And Gabriel the trumpeter, though he takes a horn, turns out to have taken a *drinking* horn, not the oxhorn of old but an artificial one made of "hammered silver." The casual announcement that Michael will "blow a little noise/ When the supper has been spread" lends a sense of impending doom. The irony in Michael the archangel's blowing a *little noise* is evident. The herald Gabriel's presence, moreover, suggests that a new era is about to unfold; and could the fish-tail symbolize a last remnant of the dying Christian epoch? Appropriately, he follows Michael into the scene; the warrior must prepare the way for the new by destroying the old. And Gabriel speaks of wonders from the "wet roads" where men—presumably dead men—walk. He speaks, that is, of life beyond death in a townland where death is not a reality. Clearly this is no ordinary dream of utopia.

The final lines, "Till he has fallen asleep/ Upon the starry brink," depict a suspension of energy; Gabriel the herald sleeps upon the *brink* of something new, the start of a new order. Hence the townland *"That is the world's bane"* may be read as an imaginative dream which prophesies the destruction of the old and the commencement of a higher order. The confusion in the poem comes because one cannot be certain of precisely what is being destroyed—the natural world or the happy townland itself. The safest solution may be that the poem represents a mere mortal's dream of perfection, a dream which is too restricted by human nature to approximate an actual description of the new and higher order; hence the rather banal image of the river of beer. Perhaps both this world and man's most utopian dreams fall short of the ideal which awaits beyond the brink on which Gabriel rests.

Far from furthering the poet's quest for unity, the GREEN HELMET poems do not even look toward reconciliation and harmony; they are for the most part blighted by hostility, anger, and remorse, and their obsessive subject is discord—either between lovers or among men. Most of the images from nature which occupied Yeats in the previous volume, several of which will return in later poems to effect the cosmic reconciliation of *A Vision*, are curiously absent from the GREEN HELMET poems; in fact, there is a dearth of distinctive imagery throughout the volume. These stark poems reveal, even more clearly than the SEVEN WOODS poems, what misery befalls a sensitive man who emerges from a private world of vision and reflection into the turbulent arena of theater management and public life in general. Such a man is more grievously burdened if at the same time his beloved lady rushes into an ill-fated marriage with another man, as Maud Gonne did in 1903. Yeats is so anxiety-ridden that he lacks the detachment to reflect upon the idealistic schemes of his imagination. The battle of opposites grips him too intensely to permit more than a forlorn expression of hope that those opposites might one day be reconciled. This anguish results in a loss of poetic power and a deeper consciousness of disunity. The far-reaching effects of this anxiety upon the poet's search for universal unity, therefore, make the GREEN HELMET poems pertinent to this discussion.

Perhaps the most unfortunate result of Yeats's sense of harassment is an intensification of the divisive social awareness noted earlier in the SEVEN WOODS poems. Annoyed by unappreciative theater audiences, inferior poets who imitated his work, and wrongheaded Irishmen in general, Yeats formulates what MacNeice calls "the cult of the Big House," [10] drawing careful distinctions between the select, aristocratic "we" and the brawling, anonymous, outside "they." No longer does he conceal his true self beneath a deceptive public mask as he did in the double-dealing SEVEN WOODS poems; dispensing with ceremonious tact, the poet attacks his opponents head-on, calling them "fools," "knaves," and "dolts," denouncing their behavior with aggressive directness. The mask image, which appears in only one poem ("The Mask"), serves to conceal a lover's true self from his (or her) lover, rather than serving the poet as a public pose.

10 Louis MacNeice, *The Poetry of W. B. Yeats* (New York: Oxford University Press, 1941), 95.

One must seek in vain for evidence that Yeats is above class snobbery, that he is able to objectify his class attitudes—a task he would find difficult even in the allegedly objective preparation of *A Vision,* wherein his preference for the aristocratic is counter- balanced by the equal strength and attraction of the "democratic" voice. This is not to say that he is disdainful of the lower classes; when he condemns the crowd in these poems, the middle class is his target. He makes his position clear in a 1907 essay: "Three types of men have made all beautiful things. Aristocracies have made beautiful manners . . . and the countrymen have made beau- tiful stories and beliefs . . . and the artists have made all the rest, because Providence has filled them with recklessness." [11] Signifi- cantly missing from the roll call is the entire middle class, though presumably a member of this class could, like Yeats himself, become an artist. Perhaps it is characteristic of Yeats's interest in polar extremes that he can find sympathy and deep affection for the lower classes and for the aristocracy; but the middle class, instead of being viewed, as it might conceivably have been, as a blend of the two, is totally alien to his temperament.

In "At Galway Races" Yeats speaks nostalgically of a time when horsemen were his companions: "Before the merchant and the clerk / Breathed on the world with timid breath." Elsewhere it is not the middle class's timidity which distresses him, but rather its boldness. He writes to Lady Gregory in "These Are the Clouds":

> These are the clouds about the fallen sun,
> The majesty that shuts his burning eye:
> The weak lay hand on what the strong has done,
> Till that be tumbled that was lifted high
> And discord follow upon unison,
> And all things at one common level lie.

11 W. B. Yeats, "Poetry and Tradition," in his *Essays and Introductions* (New York: Macmillan, 1961), 251.

Such examples abound in the GREEN HELMET volume. In "All Things Can Tempt Me," Ireland is a "fool-driven land"; and addressing Douglas Hyde ("Craoibhin Aoibhin") in "At the Abbey Theatre," Yeats views the theater audience as petulant, whimsical children whose mockery merits only mockery in return:

> You've dandled them and fed them from the book
> And know them to the bone; impart to us—
> We'll keep the secret—a new trick to please.
> Is there a bridle for this Proteus
> That turns and changes like his draughty seas?
> Or is there none, most popular of men,
> But when they mock us, that we mock again?

On the other hand, Yeats upholds the aristocratic tradition with regrettable naivete in such poems as "Upon a House Shaken by the Land Agitation"; this particular house, he says, has produced "all / That comes of the best knit to the best."

>   Although
> Mean roof-trees were the sturdier for its fall,
> How should their luck run high enough to reach
> The gifts that govern men, and after these
> To gradual Time's last gift, a written speech
> Wrought of high laughter, loveliness and ease?

Louis MacNeice, whose judgments are rather obviously colored by his own social convictions, says of Yeats: "He was still pinning his faith to the Big House, and preferring to ignore the fact that in most cases these houses maintained no culture worth speaking of—nothing but an insidious bonhomie and a way with horses. These qualities themselves, it must be admitted, came to fascinate him—an intellectual jumping his hedges by proxy." [12]

Certainly this is attacking Yeats in a very tender spot indeed; both in his association with Lady Gregory and in his somewhat

12 MacNeice, *The Poetry of W. B. Yeats*, 97.

exaggerated ancestral pretensions, Yeats often seemed to jump his hedges by proxy. But personal fault-finding is not the goal of this discussion (an understanding of Yeats's temperament may go far toward explaining and excusing his social bias); the point is that once again Yeats has been interrupted in his quest for wholeness and harmony; and personally bewildered by his experiences in the Irish theater movement, he reacts by espousing a social attitude to which he will remain faithful for the rest of his days, even when he consciously resumes his quest for reconciliation. In fairness to Yeats the point should be made that his abhorrence of the crowd is not determined purely upon social lines; his readers, his theater audiences, his imitators, his countrymen, and his business associates alike incur his arrogant and unqualified scorn, though the worst of it seems reserved for the middle class in general.

If the noisy crowd is upsetting to Yeats, it nonetheless exerts considerable influence upon his attitudes. The opening poem of the volume, "His Dream," for example, suggests that Yeats has reluctantly begun to view his poetry from the critical perspective of his secular audience. This poem is especially instructive because here the crowd does not play the antagonist as it does in almost every other poem in which it appears; instead, it plays a curiously seductive role, suggesting a certain ambivalence in Yeats's attitude. The content of the poem is quite simple: the dreamer, while rowing his "gaudy ship," sees a crowd surrounding him on the shore. The crowd rushes forward to identify a shrouded figure which rests on the deck of his ship. Because it has "such dignity of limb," the crowd calls the figure Death and begins chanting this name. Despite himself the dreamer takes up their cry, "Naming it with ecstatic breath."

Harold Bloom suggests that the "gaudy ship" may refer both to Yeats's earlier intensity of love and to his earlier poetry. Bloom cites as evidence the fact that the phrase "dignity of limb," in

Yeats's rhetoric, invariably describes Maud Gonne, and he interprets the crowd upon the shore as Yeats's friends who would urge him to recognize that Maud Gonne is a "death-principle." I would refine one of Bloom's suggestions and disprove another. Yeats himself, who explains in a note that the poem is based upon an actual dream, may have had no conscious symbolism in mind when he composed the poem; and even though "the terrible logic of nightmare" (as Bloom describes it) may equate Maud Gonne with Death in Yeats's unconscious mind, I find it difficult to see this as a poem concerning Maud Gonne at all. Admittedly this lady, with her sudden marriage and almost equally sudden separation, was much on Yeats's mind at the time these poems were written; she appears in each of the half-dozen or so poems that follow this one. But whenever she appears in Yeats's poetry, Maude Gonne is almost always viewed as maddeningly desirable but hopelessly out of reach. The shrouded figure in this poem, even though its "dignity of limb" may inspire ecstasy among those who chant its name, scarcely seems either desirable or unattainable. Moreover, we know from Yeats's private remarks as well as his poems that Maud Gonne was intensely alive, embodying the principle of the "active man" as opposed to Yeats's own inclination to be the "contemplative man," so that equating her with Death—even his own death—would seem at the very least uncharacteristic. And finally, as the object of Yeats's most enduring dream, Maud Gonne scarcely requires symbolic representation. Because she appears as a woman in so many of these poems, it would seem pointless for her to be disguised as the mysteriously shrouded figure in this one.

Bloom's other suggestion, that the ship may refer to Yeats's earlier poetry, seems more suitable, though I would argue that it is the ship's *cargo* and not the ship itself which is symbolic. As the SEVEN WOODS poems showed, Yeats has become increasingly conscious of his audience; the crowd upon the shore seems to function not as admonitory friends but rather as anonymous onlookers—in short, as an audience. Hence the cargo displayed upon the deck might logically represent Yeats's poetry.[13] That the figure is shrouded may suggest Yeats's growing consciousness of the decadent aspect of some of his earlier poetry, such as the death-music of THE WIND AMONG THE REEDS. That the figure is called by the *sweet* name of Death, and that the dreamer chants with *ecstatic* breath may suggest the persistent allure of this kind of poetry even when its decadent aspect has been recognized. What is interesting here is the ambivalence of the speaker's attitude; at first he seeks to hush the crowd, then he joins their cry reluctantly, and finally he yields himself to ecstasy.

The poem is an appropriate beginning for the GREEN HELMET volume, for it marks the poet's unwilling admittance to the crowd upon the shore. He has taken up the cry of the crowd, and despite his ecstasy the word he chants is *Death*. The entire volume reflects this sense of confusion concerning his relationship with the crowd. Not yet equipped with the intricate series of personality types, explainable by moon phase, which were to be included in *A Vision*, Yeats is like a drowning man in a sea of hostile personalities, from Maud Gonne to the stranger who attends his plays.

Another result of Yeats's collision with public life which will have dramatic effects upon his quest for unity is his attempt to extract himself from the turbulence and diversity of such life in order to objectify his attitudes. Although this theme emerges only a few times in the GREEN HELMET volume, it is significant, for only through an objective distillation of his personality can Yeats eventually achieve a harmonious conjunction of opposite personalities. The more fully dramatized "I" of the later poems is both aesthetically and philosophically superior to the undramatized, naked "I" of the GREEN HELMET poems.

Nowhere is the impulse toward self-distillation better expressed than in the short poem "The Coming of Wisdom with Time":

13 Bloom, *Yeats*, 168–69.

> Though leaves are many, the root is one;
> Through all the lying days of my youth
> I swayed my leaves and flowers in the sun;
> Now I may wither into the truth.

One risks spoiling such compression and beauty by commentary, but through the tree metaphor Yeats expresses his wish to retreat from the outer world in order to sink into the "truth" of the concealed self, the basic self. The poem is sometimes read to mean simply that wisdom comes with time, as the title states; but by identifying himself with the tree, Yeats suggests that the wisdom to be gained is an insight into his own being and that the truth of his being lies not in the diversity of the outer personality but in the hard simplicity of the basic, inner self.

An example of Yeats's impulse toward objectivity is "The Mask," in which one lover (presumably the lady, though there is no real evidence either way) asks the other to remove his mask; but he refuses on the grounds that it was the mask, and not his real face behind it, which won her heart. The lady persists, eager to learn whether the mask is deceptive:

> 'But lest you are my enemy,
> I must enquire.'
> 'O no, my dear, let all that be;
> What matter, so there is but fire
> In you, in me?'

The result is a justification of the false face and especially of the kind of detachment which enables one to play the games of life and love more skillfully, a detachment that the speaker had lacked in the earlier SEVEN WOODS poem, "Never Give All the Heart." Such a justification, however, is likely to leave the reader unconvinced, as there is a note of bitter irony in the poem, as if the lover regrets, even as he defends his mask, the necessity of wearing it. The conclusion underscores this irony when the masked lover dismisses the question of the mask: " 'What matter, so there is but fire / In you, in me?' " For the opening line of the poem describes the mask as *"burning* gold," and the lady has sought " 'To find if hearts be wild and wise, / And yet not *cold'* " (italics mine). Perhaps the usefulness of this particular mask has been to shield a cold heart; and if this is so, the only "fire" is in the mask itself.

In "All Things Can Tempt Me," Yeats moves somewhat closer to his later conception of the mask as the opposite self which one must pursue in order to achieve wholeness and harmony within the self. In the poem just discussed, as in all previous ones employing the image of the mask, Yeats uses the mask as a mere shield against the kind of personal commitment that could result in pain or, to say approximately the same thing with different emphasis, as a means of dissociating and objectifying the self. In "All Things Can Tempt Me," he does not use the mask image directly; but he does recognize the persistent attraction of the opposite self, and the mask is implicit:

> All things can tempt me from this craft of verse:
> One time it was a woman's face, or worse—
> The seeming needs of my fool-driven land;
> Now nothing but comes readier to the hand
> Than this accustomed toil. When I was young,
> I had not given a penny for a song
> Did not the poet sing it with such airs
> That one believed he had a sword upstairs;
> Yet would be now, could I but have my wish,
> Colder and dumber and deafer than a fish.

The poets whom he admired in his youth had burning masks; even though they may have had no sword upstairs, they *sang* as if they had, and this was their appeal. But now that he has adopted such a mask, now that he himself has written as if he had a sword upstairs, he is drawn by the opposite attraction—coldness, dumbness, even deafness. It is tempting to diagram this attraction by anticipating Yeats's later image of the opposing gyres: the young man begins at some neutral point and pursues the burning mask;

then, when he has advanced as far in that direction as possible, he shifts direction toward the *cold* mask, and the burning mask begins to wane.

This poem has suffered, I believe, from a general tendency to misread its fourth line, resulting in a mistaken interpretation of the whole poem. The general view, which is endorsed by Unterecker and Bloom among others, can be paraphrased thus: Once, Maud Gonne and Ireland distracted me from writing verse; but now nothing comes more readily to my hand than writing. Such a reading fails on three counts. First, the title and the opening line do not permit the assumption that the temptations occurred only in the past; the poet says that all things *can* tempt him, not just that they once *could*. Second, one must remember that the fourth line reads, "nothing *but* comes readier to the hand," and not, as most commentators seem to assume, "nothing comes readier to the hand." If my reading is accurate, the poem states that *everything* comes more readily to the poet's hand than his "accustomed toil" of writing verse. The third consideration which reinforces my reading is that the first full stop in the poem occurs in the fifth line, dividing the poem into two parts at that point rather than at the end of the third line. The first part of the poem traces the steady progression of the temptations up to the present time; the second part examines the present temptation to abandon poetry altogether, to become "Colder and dumber and deafer than a fish." Thus the poem does not suggest, as Bloom assumes, that Yeats "begins to sense a new self-mastery in his craft"; rather, he is wholly impatient with that obsessive craft and longs to escape it. Obviously this reading poses Yeats in a more radical posture than previous readings have done, and it gives fuller weight to the astonishing and powerful final line of the poem.[14]

14 Unterecker, *A Reader's Guide*, 110; Bloom, *Yeats*, 170.

Such consciousness of disunity within the self corresponds to the overall emphasis upon discord throughout the volume. Only if one optimistically views awareness of the conflict of opposites as a necessary preliminary to an eventual reconciliation of those opposites can he interpret the GREEN HELMET poems as signs of progress. I am more inclined to see them as a setback, in regard to both reconciliation of opposites, and aesthetic beauty. Despite such praiseworthy poems as "No Second Troy" and "The Coming of Wisdom with Time," this volume makes a poor showing for an artist of Yeats's stature. He seems to reach very low, as if to discover the lowest common denominator of his poetry, with a small stock of forceful imagery or symbolism, a flatness of overall effect, and a disappointing lack of courage and affirmation.

John Unterecker has admired the interlinking of these poems through key words such as *thought* or *blame*, which, appropriately, consist of ordinary conversational terms rather than images; the word *blame*, for example, begins "No Second Troy" and connects it with the opening line of the following poem, "Reconciliation." Unterecker sees this device as a means of integrating the separate poems into "a kind of lyrical narrative." I am more inclined to condemn these links as a self-conscious and arbitrary attempt at some form of thematic unity which Yeats never achieves in this volume. Too often the verbal links seem merely coincidental, as when the line "I had not given a penny" in "All Things Can Tempt Me" links that poem with "Brown Penny," the closing poem. The difference is precisely the same as that between organic form and imposed from.[15]

Holding his own poetry as well as his fellow man in such bitter contempt, Yeats manages to affirm little in these poems: the tradi-

15 Unterecker, *A Reader's Guide*, 104.

tion of aristocracy, as we have seen, and in the final poem the necessity for love, which may be intended as a correction to the overall bitterness of the volume:

> O love is the crooked thing,
> There is nobody wise enough
> To find out all that is in it,
> For he would be thinking of love
> Till the stars had run away
> And the shadows eaten the moon.
> Ah, penny, brown penny, brown penny,
> One cannot begin it too soon.

Yet, characteristically, even in acknowledging the necessity for love, Yeats must point out that love is "the crooked thing," the ambivalent power that is beyond man's capacity for full understanding.

5

RESPONSIBILITIES
The Poet as
Visionary Reformer

HAVING DESCENDED into the hell of public life and unrequited love, Yeats manages in his next collection of poems, RESPONSI-BILITIES (1914), to resurrect himself from the defensive, half-despairing nay-saying of the GREEN HELMET poems. Not only is RESPONSIBILITIES Yeats's finest piece of work since THE WIND AMONG THE REEDS, it is on the whole more vigorous, versatile, and affirmative than anything he had written previously. The versatility of approaches alone is impressive: there are occasional poems, such as those written in the fever of the Hugh Lane pictures controversy; visionary poems such as "The Cold Heaven" and "The Magi"; satirical poems directed against the Paudeens (Yeats's term for a philistine breed of Irish storekeepers or, by extension, for their social class); epigrams; and the characteristic stock of love poems and meditative poems. The poet's mood throughout is highly personal, deeply committed, emotional, combative, and urgent. Not since THE ROSE has he expressed so vigorous and determined an effort to resolve the perplexing conflicts of human life, and certainly he comes closer to such a resolution in this volume than ever before.

After such a recent temptation to succumb to the wretched-
ness he experienced in the workaday world and to give up poetry
altogether, it is a welcome change to find Yeats reaffirming his
faith in visionary revelation and the solid substance of his art.
He now appears to view himself as an essential mediator between
the private world of vision and the public world of reality, his
function being to reconcile these conflicting worlds through the
revealed wisdom of his poetry. He demonstrates his determination to effect such a reconciliation by using two quotations as
epigraphs to affirm the importance of dream but at the same
time acknowledge its necessary relation to reality:

> *'In dreams begins responsibility.'*

> *'How am I fallen from myself, for a long time now*
> *I have not seen the Prince of Chang in my dreams.'*

As the first quotation suggests and the following poems confirm,
an artist's dream imposes upon him the responsibility to communicate his vision of an ideal world to the real world which
falls short of that vision. The lessons of Shelley's "A Defense
of Poetry" have not been lost upon Yeats: "Poetry . . . arrests
the vanishing apparitions which haunt the interlunations of life,
and veiling them, or in language or in form, sends them forth
among mankind. . . . Poetry redeems from decay the visitations
of the divinity in man."

The second epigraph comments upon a division within the
poet's self and implies his need to reunify that self. The absence
of the Prince of Chang from recent dreams closely parallels a
passage in the untitled closing poem of the volume, in which Yeats
speaks of the ghostly communicator:

> *that reed-throated whisperer,*
> *Who comes at need, although not now as once*
> *A clear articulation in the air,*
> *But inwardly.*

By framing the RESPONSIBILITIES poems with the epigraphs and this unnamed poem, Yeats may wish to indicate an advance in attitude concerning the sources of mystic wisdom. At the outset he senses a lack of visionary communication; at the end he perceives that such a communication must come not merely from dreams, not from an outside source (*"A clear articulation in the air"*), but ultimately from his own inner resources. The responsibility is his—to seek, to discover, and finally to communicate.

Merely communicating his visions of perfection to the busy and frequently hostile world of men, however, guarantees no change in the order of things; much, much more is required of the poet—hence the plural form of the volume's title. What, then, are the specific responsibilities which Yeats's visionary wisdom imposes upon him? In such a diverse collection of poems there are, as one might expect, multiple answers; and at times these answers seem to qualify and even to contradict each other, as it was impossible for Yeats to sustain for long any kind of didacticism beyond the hard core of his basic convictions. As in his earlier poems, no sooner does he make a pronouncement than he begins to qualify, to reconsider, and often to overturn. In the midst of his excoriating attacks upon William Murphy and other Paudeens who took the opposite side in the Lane controversy, Yeats typically feels compelled to seek a creative pattern or framework that contains *all* of mankind—aristocrats, artists, and Paudeens alike: "There cannot be, confusion of our sound forgot, / A single soul that lacks a sweet crystalline cry."

Having acknowledged his personal ideal of unity and order throughout creation, Yeats resumes his attack on Murphy ("an old foul mouth") and the rest once again in "To a Shade." What matters is not that Yeats may seem inconsistent in alternately denouncing and embracing various members of his race; what matters is that he manages to express faith in unity at the same time that he is conscious of disunity. He can wage battle against the middle class without despair, without pinning his hopes for improvement upon the deadly arrival of the apocalypse, without losing sight of his imagination's conviction that unity does, after all, exist beyond the turbulence of everyday strife. This, surely, indicates a more comprehensive insight and a closer step toward reconciliation of the opposing worlds of the real and the ideal.

Raymond Cowell succinctly describes the kinship of this volume with the rest of Yeats's work: "The characteristic Yeatsian temptations—aristocratic disdain, aesthetic or mystical remoteness, jewelled rhetoric, nostalgic romanticism—are still present in this period, but the resistance to them is increasingly honest, even heroic. Indeed he was never to leave these and related temptations completely behind him, for in a very important sense all Yeats's poetry is a poetry of temptation."[1] Temptations are indeed persistent, but in these poems Yeats is at his combative best; and the violent clashing of swords is a refreshing change from the wails of anguish which characterized the immediately preceding volumes.

To settle upon a single governing purpose behind the diverse RESPONSIBILITIES poems would inevitably result in oversimplification, though, as I have suggested, the dominant thrust of the volume is toward reforming the world by introducing to it the wisdom—both mystic and mundane—of the poet. Even if certain individual poems, such as the love poems, bear no obvious relation to this goal, most do deal with this form of reconciliation. They reveal Yeats's sense of a worldly mission, one that extends far beyond the self-centered lamentations of the GREEN HELMET volume to include the social, political, and spiritual reform of the Irish people.

One way of safeguarding the future of Ireland is to make certain that she preserves the best qualities of her own past. Yeats's sense of the past was always strong and appreciative, and it seems to become even more so when he confronts the bigotry and small-

1 Raymond Cowell, *W. B. Yeats* (London: Arco, 1969), 37.

ness of mind of the Paudeens who oppose him in the Lane controversy, who have sent Charles Stewart Parnell to an early grave, and who violently condemn the production of John Millington Synge's *The Playboy of the Western World* in Yeats's theater. It would be a more than twice-told tale to enumerate the many influences which led Yeats to explore the mythological past of his country, but in RESPONSIBILITIES more than previously he draws from Irish myth and Irish history to find parallels to contemporary conflicts and to teach therefrom a valuable lesson or two. It is important to note that he explores the past in order to prepare for the future and not merely to lament bygone glories. His mood is considerably more urgent than nostalgic.

Yeats acknowledges his responsibility to the historic past in the untitled prefatory poem, in which he addresses and briefly describes certain of his ancestors, and asks them to

> *Pardon that for a barren passion's sake,*
> *Although I have come close on forty-nine,*
> *I have no child, I have nothing but a book,*
> *Nothing but that to prove your blood and mine.*

The respect and pride which Yeats expresses for the past and his ancestors in this poem is quite genuine, but it is nevertheless tempered by irony. Despite the words he speaks, everything we know of Yeats confirms that he would consider having *"nothing but a book"* to offer, a very fine thing indeed. There is possibly a deliberate resemblance between his plea for pardon and the popular Renaissance custom among penurious writers of asking a rich patron's pardon for dedicating such inferior work to him, a custom often inspired by no nobler a motive than greed. In denigrating the achievement of his book Yeats is exploiting the spuriousness of the plea for pardon; and by making use of the device at a time when he is no longer supported by the tradition, he manages both to preserve history and to update the tradition. The emphasis of the repetition in the closing lines, "*I have nothing but a book, / Nothing but that,*" makes it clear that Yeats considers his book a worthy contribution indeed.[2]

Unfortunately, the poem also reveals a less admirable side of Yeats's respect for the past: his class snobbery. In his book of memoirs, *Ave*, George Moore pours scalding water on Yeats's family pretensions, wondering "why Willie Yeats should feel himself called upon to denounce the class to which he himself belonged essentially."[3] The first and last poems of RESPONSIBILI-TIES are thought to have been inspired by Moore's attack, the justice of which is amply demonstrated in much that Yeats said and wrote at this time—for example, the following diary entry: "I have been told that the crudity common to all the Moores came from the mother's family—Mayo squireens probably half peasants in education and occupation."[4] In the poem under consideration he boasts of the

> Merchant and scholar who have left me blood
> That has not passed through any huckster's loin,

a passage which directly contradicts his earlier sneer at merchants in "At Galway Races" (GREEN HELMET). As Jeffares amusingly points out, the word *merchant* is affected by its companions; an ordinary merchant is contemptible, but a merchant *kinsman* is a person of worth![5]

Bloom is less inclined to smile at Yeats's social attitudes. He

2 Biographical information imposes a second irony upon Yeats's regretting that he has "no child . . . nothing but a book" to offer his ancestors. During the period when he was composing the RESPONSIBILITIES poems, a young woman with whom he had had a love affair sent a telegram to Coole announcing her pregnancy, and Yeats frantically interpreted the message as an attempt to trick him into marriage. But for the fact that the lady was bluffing, Yeats might in 1914 have had something more to offer than a book! (My sources for this incident are Norman Jeffares, *W. B. Yeats: Man and Poet* [2nd ed.; New York: Barnes and Noble, 1966], 175; and Richard Ellmann, *Yeats: The Man and the Masks* [New York: Dutton, 1948], 208.)

3 Quoted in Jeffares, *W. B. Yeats: Man and Poet*, 179.

4 Yeats's diary, quoted by Jeffares, *W. B. Yeats: Man and Poet*, 180.

5 Jeffares, *W. B. Yeats: Man and Poet*, 181.

questions whether "to prove your blood and mine" is an appropriate poetic function in our age even though it may have been in the Renaissance and in the time of Pindar: "The *sprezzatura* of one age too readily becomes the mindlessness of another, and those such as Yeats, who would hold back the tide, are battered by it."[6] This criticism seems unfair in view of Yeats's purpose. If he is to be battered by the tide in seeking to uphold the aristocratic traditions of the past, his attempt is no less heroic for ending in defeat (one recalls Cuchulain engaging in precisely the same heroic struggle, though for other reasons). Certainly Yeats was snobbish, and certainly—as MacNeice puts it—he jumps his hedges by proxy; but his interest in his own family history and in the aristocratic traditions of the past has deeper roots than a mere puffing of his own dignity. His new experiences with the philistines, in theater work and elsewhere, have inspired new respect for the gentler traditions of the past. And he seeks to fulfill his personal sense of historic continuity by extolling the old, aristocratic way of life and by preserving whatever he can of that life for the benefit of the present generation.

"The Grey Rock" demonstrates Yeats's firm commitment to the historic and mythological past of his country, and it introduces a theme which is to become increasingly important to Yeats: the repetitive patterns of human history. Having addressed his ancestors in the prefatory poem, he now addresses his deceased literary friends from the Rhymers' Club in London. Imagining that an old story will please them more than "stories now in fashion," he recounts the mythological Aoife's lament before an assembly of gods at Slievenamon. Aoife announces that her mortal lover has renounced her gift of longevity and has chosen to die; for, having seen his king's son wounded in battle, he is unwilling to enjoy supernatural health when his lord

6 Harold Bloom, *Yeats* (New York: Oxford University Press, 1970), 171.

must suffer and die. When Aoife finishes her story, the gods pour wine over her head,

> And she with Goban's wine adrip,
> No more remembering what had been,
> Stared at the gods with laughing lip.

Yeats structures the poem to represent five time periods, each set behind the other: the present (Yeats tells the story), the historic past (the now-deceased poets of the Rhymers' Club), and three periods within the mythological past (the assembly of gods at Slievenamon, the earlier battle with the Danes, and the even earlier promise of Aoife to her lover). This tale-within-a-tale structure contributes a strong sense of continuity between past and present.

Yeats merges past and present thematically in three ways. First, when Aoife rends her clothes and asks why the faithful heart must always love the false, she voices a dilemma that is no less perplexing in the present than in the mythological past which she inhabits:

> Why should the faithfullest heart most love
> The bitter sweetness of false faces?
> Why must the lasting love what passes,
> Why are the gods by men betrayed?

The reader of *A Vision* will recognize in this speech the familiar theme of the unending attraction and conflict of opposites.

The second way Yeats merges past and present is through the exaltation of art as a means of reconciling man to his condition, then and now. The moment when the gods stand and pour wine over Aoife's head is a ritualistic ceremony, a holy anointing. Like the sacrament of baptism, which removes the taint of original sin from the soul, "Goban's wine" removes the taint of memory; and like the wine of holy communion, "Goban's wine" restores the spirit to a condition of blessedness. Art, as symbolized by the hammered silver cup and the magic sacramental wine, joins

Aoife to that holy company of those who devote themselves to the religion of art: the gods, the Rhymers' Club poets, and Yeats himself. (To exalt the artist and his patrons as well, Yeats tells us that "only the gods" are permitted to buy Goban's "sacred stuff," which he brews and pours into cups which were "hammered out on mountain top" at a time "when frenzy stirred his thews.")

When we read the poem in this way, Aoife's story, too, adds dimension to the theme of the sanctity of art. Murrough, the king's son, has died from battle wounds; but Aoife's lover has died an even nobler death, having first dispelled the Danish troops with a shout which caused panic among them, then having freely chosen to die rather than to live when his own prince lay wounded. Perhaps it is not too farfetched to see in the panic-inducing shout of Aoife's noble lover a reflection of the power of art, in particular the power of the *word*. For Murrough and his best soldiers had been unable to conquer the Danish army and would have perished on the battlefield but for that "shouting of an unseen man," who proves to be Aoife's lover. The word, not the sword, dispels the Danes. Yeats may well have this in mind when he speaks at the end of the poem in his own voice once again, scorning those who exalt the sword over "lover's music":

> *I have kept my faith, though faith was tried,*
> *To that rock-born, rock-wandering foot,*
> *And the world's altered since you died,*
> *And I am in no good repute*
> *With the loud host before the sea,*
> *That think sword-strokes were better meant*
> *Than lover's music—let that be,*
> *So that the wandering foot's content.*

The passage is reminiscent of the closing poem of THE ROSE, "To Ireland in the Coming Times":

> *Nor may I less be counted one*
> *With Davis, Mangan, Ferguson,*
> *Because, to him who ponders well,*
> *My rhymes more than their rhyming tell*
> *Of things discovered in the deep,*
> *Where only body's laid asleep.*

Now, as then, Yeats is convinced that his art can serve his country even if Ireland does not recognize the value of his contribution.

Finally, past and present merge in the poem through the analogies which Yeats draws between the living and the dead and, further back still, the mythological dead. The immortal Aoife is balanced, in her love for a mortal, by a reference to the actress Florence Farr ("a woman whom none could please"), who yearned for men like gods.[7] The drunken gods in the poem are parallel to the Cheshire Cheese poets in two ways: in the amusing sense that both are drinkers at their respective taverns, and in the more serious sense that both have become intoxicated by art, eating and drinking from the deep, hammered silver that Goban crafted. And Aoife's lover, who renounces the favors of the gods and thereby surpasses them in nobility of spirit, resembles the poet who renounces the applause he might otherwise win from his country and serves best through his poetry.

The Lane pictures controversy supplies Yeats with an occasion for addressing a more pointed lesson from the past to his own contemporaries. Hugh Lane, Lady Gregory's nephew, had offered his collection of modern paintings to the city of Dublin, provided that the city establish a permanent gallery to house them. After considerable squabbling over the design and construction of the gallery, the paintings wound up at the National Gallery in London, with Dublin agitating for their return. In the midst of the controversy a wealthy man offered a second gift of money to the gallery fund if the public's wish for the gallery could

7 Cited by John Unterecker, *A Reader's Guide to William Butler Yeats* (New York: Noonday Press, 1959), 115, among others.

be demonstrated. Yeats replies in one of his most scathing poems, "To a Wealthy Man Who Promised a Second Subscription to the Dublin Municipal Gallery If It Were Proved the People Wanted Pictures," which begins:

> You gave, but will not give again
> Until enough of Paudeen's pence
> By Biddy's halfpennies have lain
> To be 'some sort of evidence,'
> Before you'll put your guineas down,
> That things it were a pride to give
> Are what the blind and ignorant town
> Imagines best to make it thrive.

Yeats cites for the education of this half-hearted patron of the arts three patrons of history—Ercole, Duke of Ferrara; Guidobaldo, Duke of Urbino; and Cosimo de Medici—who made their contributions without regard for the opinions of onion-sellers, shepherds, and the like. The modern patron, Yeats insists, must emulate these men in order to "breed the best" for the future, to supply "the right twigs for an eagle's nest." As in the preceding poem, Yeats considers that the public, being "blind and ignorant," cannot know what is best for it; but the artist and the aristocrat, that blessed pair whom Yeats celebrates all his days, must make their offerings heedless of indifference or blame.

But the lesson of history which Yeats most insists upon seems directed neither to the aristocrat nor to the artist, but to the whole generation of Irishmen. The stuff of heroes, Yeats argues, is the generous gesture, the expense of action without calculating gains or losses. As Yeats's grandfather William Pollexfen had often said to him (as recorded in the prefatory poem), *Only the wasteful virtues earn the sun.* In "September 1913" the poet mourns the consequences of a failure to join modern Ireland with the old heroism. A new and decidedly lesser breed of Irishmen has arisen, one that seems "born to pray and save." Romantic Ireland—as embodied in such great men as Edward Fitzgerald,

Robert Emmet, Wolfe Tone, and Yeats's old hero John O'Leary
—is "dead and gone." Such men had little time to pray and little
to save, but they "have gone about the world like wind," weighing
lightly their great contributions.

Thomas Parkinson sees "the relation between the daily mood
and the moment of exaltation" as the chief focus of Yeats's poetic
intent in these poems, and certainly a good argument can be made
for this position.[8] Yeats's recommendation of passionate, exalted,
and generous living and his loathing of the petty, the niggardly,
and the self-serving gain much force from the precedent of Irish
heroes, both historical and mythological. In the last of the Hugh
Lane poems, "To a Shade," Yeats addresses the ghost of Parnell
and warns him not to re-visit Dublin, where "an old foul mouth"
(presumably William Martin Murphy) has set "the pack" against
a man like himself (Lane). Lane, like the romantic heroes, is
of the "passionate serving kind"; but Ireland disowns him as it
has disowned Parnell.

Even in denouncing his enemies as representative of modern
Ireland, however, Yeats does not forsake his conviction that better
days are coming; somehow, despite the greedy, snarling pack of
Paudeens, the artists and their aristocratic patrons will usher in
a future that is more compatible with the glorious past. But what
is to sustain these saviors in the meantime? One solution, as presented in "The Grey Rock," is the consolation of art, which is
capable of extinguishing anguish and the thirst for vengeance. A
second solution, more representative of Parkinson's "relation between the daily mood and the moment of exaltation," is the attainment of tragic joy, which is an insight into primary causes so
profound that it liberates one from anguish and expresses itself in
laughter. The poet advises Lady Gregory ("To a Friend Whose
Work Has Come to Nothing") to "Be secret and take defeat,"

8 Thomas Parkinson, *W. B. Yeats, Self-Critic: A Study of His Early
Verse* (Berkeley: University of California Press, 1951), 105.

since she, "Being honour bred," cannot compete with the pack of liars who would lose nothing even if they were proven liars.

> Bred to a harder thing
> Than Triumph, turn away
> And like a laughing string
> Whereon mad fingers play
> Amid a place of stone,
> Be secret and exult,
> Because of all things known
> That is most difficult.

The forbidding proximity of madness to this strange exultation makes it seem an attitude more easily recommended than adopted. The analogy equates Lady Gregory with the laughing string, and her persecutors with the "mad fingers" which play upon that string; but one who exhibits joy amidst acute suffering is likely to appear mad even if the actual madness resides only in the persecutor.

What is most striking about this prescription is that Yeats, confronting the familiar conflict of opposites (in this case, the crowd versus the aristocrat), recommends the pursuit of emotions opposite to the natural, spontaneous ones—that is, he recommends a mask. Instead of grieving over one's woes, one embraces joy. And since this emotional triumph is possible only in defeat (*i.e.*, if one's "work has come to nothing"), still another juxtaposition of opposites occurs. Yeats is working steadily toward a comprehensive and systematic means of dealing with the conflict of opposites.

The theme of tragic joy came to interest Yeats more and more and is dealt with perhaps most brilliantly in "Lapis Lazuli" (from LAST POEMS) many years after the writing of RESPONSI-BILITIES; but the theme receives a delightful treatment in "The Three Hermits," a poem which resembles "Lapis Lazuli" in several ways and in fact seems, in retrospect, a direct anticipation of the later poem. In "The Three Hermits" those who are em-

broiled in worldly experience contrast with those who transcend
it through the mystical attainment of tragic joy. One hermit, dutifully praying, is frustrated because he falls asleep when he should
pray longer; he represents the struggle of the spirit with the flesh,
but in struggling against his fleshly self he proves himself alien
to Yeats, who favors fulfillment, not denial, of both the earthly
and the spiritual self. The second hermit, who rummages for a
flea while deliberating upon the afterlife of human souls, is like
the first in being bound to the earth while his imagination struggles
with issues that lie beyond the earthly. The body, demanding its
sleep and being plagued by fleas, is unable to relinquish the two
hermits' aspiring spirits.

But the third hermit, unnoticed by the others and not noticing
them, either, "Giddy with his hundredth year, / Sang unnoticed
like a bird." It is clear that only this last hermit wins Yeats's approval. As Unterecker says, "That he sings like a bird should be
enough to pin him down as something near saint. That he is unnoticed in his singing assures it. Unlike the others, he has already
achieved that visionary gaiety which Yeats regarded as the special
property of blessedness." [9]

Despite the lighthearted tone of the poem (which reinforces
Yeats's approval of the third hermit's gaiety), Yeats does not
dismiss the first two hermits, much less the third. Each of them
represents a stage in Yeats's own thinking: the first, despite his
ill-advised effort to renounce the flesh, is right to expect that
something awaits the human soul beyond the "Door of Death";
the second adds to this his own conviction that beyond death is
the "Door of Birth"—that is, reincarnation—which offers holy
men a second chance; and the third hermit, plagued by neither
fleas nor sleepiness nor philosophical speculation, transcends his
environment and delights in his own secret wisdom.

Characteristically, Yeats associates tragic joy with the aristo-

9 Unterecker, *A Reader's Guide*, 122.

crat ("To a Friend Whose Work Has Come to Nothing"), the
hermit ("The Three Hermits"), and the artist ("The Peacock"),
but never with the middle class. It seems inconceivable that one
of the tribe of hucksters could be included among the elect; indeed, it is their world that is transcended through tragic joy. In
"The Peacock" Yeats scorns the pursuit of riches and exalts the
artist thus:

> What's riches to him
> That has made a great peacock
> With the pride of his eye?
> The wind-beaten, stone-grey,
> And desolate Three Rock
> Would nourish his whim.
> Live he or die
> Amid wet rocks and heather,
> His ghost will be gay
> Adding feather to feather
> For the pride of his eye.

Where the artist, the aristocrat, and the hermit must acquire
their triumphant gaiety remains mysterious; evidently an act of
will is a necessary step toward it, and presumably the several ac-
counts of visionary experiences in RESPONSIBILITIES are meant to
suggest that joy comes from insight, which arrives in turn through
vision. In "The Grey Rock," Aoife asks the assembly of gods:

> 'Why are they faithless when their might
> Is from the holy shades that rove
> The grey rock and the windy light?'

The power of mortals comes from those who inhabit the "windy
light," and the poems that present the moment of vision reinforce
Aoife's judgment by describing vision in terms of wind and light.
In "Paudeen," for example, the speaker—indignant at the "obscure spite" of shopkeepers—stumbles along "under morning
light":

> Until a curlew cried and in the luminous wind
> A curlew answered; and suddenly thereupon I thought
> That on the lonely height where all are in God's eye,
> There cannot be, confusion of our sound forgot,
> A single soul that lacks a sweet crystalline cry.

Here the "windy light" is described in reverse as a "luminous wind"; and the crying of two birds, another favorite motif often associated with vision, leads toward the speaker's realization that all creation, including the spiteful Paudeens, is ordered and precise. One has but to compare this poem with those bitter outcries from previous volumes, such as "At the Abbey Theatre," "These Are the Clouds," "The Withering of the Boughs," or any number of others, to realize how far Yeats has progressed toward the imaginative reconciliation of the real and the ideal. His visionary insight no longer suggests to him, as it so often had in the past, that the ideal world must belong exclusively to the artist, his aristocratic patrons, and perhaps certain of the peasantry. If these remain the Yeatsian elect, at least the poet has a renewed faith in a comprehensive order of creation. The implication of these poems is that with the arrival of further insight the poet will be able to perceive the precise role of even his enemies in a benevolently ordered scheme of creation.

"The Hour Before Dawn" offers another account of visionary experience and an equally forceful instance of Yeats's increasingly comprehensive point of view. The poem narrates the adventure of a "cursing rogue with a merry face" (the kind of simple peasant character of whom Yeats is increasingly fond) who seeks shelter in a "windy place" until the coming of dawn. The setting— isolated, windy, and rich in Irish folklore associations—is appropriate for vision; and the idea of awaiting dawn may suggest readiness for visionary enlightenment. As the traveler prepares his bed, he encounters a "great lad with a beery face" who sleeps away the centuries under a pile of rocks and sips beer "from Goban's mountain-top" (which may symbolize art, as "Goban's wine" did in "The Grey Rock"). This strange man, whether symbolic of the aesthete, the dreamer, both, or neither, argues for the pleasure in nothingness; he has apparently lost his interest in normal living since he came to realize that "all life longs for the Last Day."

But the traveler denounces this seemingly pessimistic philosophy, protesting that such a viewpoint would rob his life of all pleasure. He gives the other man a great pummelling and flees from the windy place just as "The clouds were brightening with the dawn." Although some have argued that Yeats favors the traveler's attitude, those who see the poem as an unresolved clash of opposites seem to have the better of the argument. Ellmann, for example, warns that the poem does not really conclude that it is better to sleep forever or to stay awake for a lifetime.[10] In my judgment, Yeats implies that both men are partially right. The sleeper's perception of life's ultimate goal corresponds to Yeats's own view as expressed in *A Vision* and in various of the later poems; but if the sleeper's insight is accurate, his response to it seems totally undesirable: shutting himself off from life and using art ("beer from Goban's mountain-top") as a means of escape. His concealment within rocks is especially revealing, since rocks symbolize for Yeats a fanatical resistance to change and, thus, to life itself (as in the later "Easter 1916"). But the traveler scarcely represents the Yeatsian ideal, either. He is resistant to the insight offered him, which is bad; but he chooses a life of activity and pleasure, which is good. The familiar clash of the contemplative man and the man of action, instead of being resolved, ends in a careful balance. That dawn arrives at the end is somewhat puzzling; the traveler appears to have gained no particular insight, though the coming of dawn, if symbolic, would seem to suggest otherwise. Perhaps the dawn functions to point out the *failure* to gain insight: a mere physical light which releases

10 Ellmann, *Yeats: The Man and the Masks,* 202.

the traveler from fear, as opposed to a spiritual light which might have altered his life radically.

Two other poems, "The Cold Heaven" and "The Magi," describe actual visions of a more elevated and mystical nature than any of those previously discussed. "The Cold Heaven," the favorite RESPONSIBILITIES poem of many critics, is a brilliantly condensed account of a vision of terror, though the exact meaning of the vision has proven elusive. The poet glances toward the sky and has a momentary vision of burning ice, a juxtaposition of opposites reminiscent of Samuel Taylor Coleridge's vision of "Kubla Khan." At once Yeats's vision drives his heart and imagination "wild"; this word, according to T. R. Henn, has overtones in Irish idiom of fierceness, gaiety, abnormal conduct, energy, and sexual power—all of which may well have a bearing upon this poem.[11] The poet's mind is emptied of everything except memories of his wretched experience in love, for which he assumes the blame "out of all sense and reason,"

> Until I cried and trembled and rocked to and fro,
> Riddled with light. Ah! when the ghost begins to quicken,
> Confusion of the death-bed over, is it sent
> Out naked on the roads, as the books say, and stricken
> By the injustice of the skies for punishment?

Like the later system of *A Vision*, the poem begins with an apprehension of the paradoxical union of contraries: the burning ice that was all the more ice because it was burning. This suggests a dynamic form of reconciliation, perceived not rationally but imaginatively: coldness intensifying because of the presence of heat. The gyres of *A Vision* operate in the same manner: the tension between the intermingling primary and antithetical tinctures causes the dynamism of both. Without the presence of the

11 T. R. Henn, *The Lonely Tower: Studies in the Poetry of W. B. Yeats* (London: Methuen & Co., 1950), 94.

opposite tincture (as in Phase 15 of the lunar phases), there is no motion, no life—only incomprehensible purity and stasis.

Here the union of fire and ice brings the Maud Gonne experience to Yeats's mind, and the images are associated with the *hot* blood of youth and the condition of the lover's soul after death. Unterecker assumes that the hot-blooded youth is balanced by "the freezing naked soul of a dead old man," [12] but the poem does not reveal the condition of the dead man's soul. Is it not more likely, in fact, that "memories that *should* be out of season / With the hot blood of youth" suggest that the old man is every bit as "hot-blooded" as the youth, though "out of season"? Perhaps Yeats, in his enduring passion for Maud Gonne, is parallel to the "burning ice" of the vision, a "freezing fire" that is all the more fire because it is freezing—all the more desirous of Maud Gonne because he is denied her.

Possibly such a reading makes too much of the interplay of opposites; or worse, perhaps it imposes too rational an order upon a visionary experience, one which Yeats described as an actual event in his life. Nevertheless, the vision of opposites seems to demand a parallel in the memory which the vision evokes. And to isolate burning youth from cold dead man is to ignore the *interplay* of fire and ice in the central imagery of the poem.

Perhaps the most impressive element in the poem is the evocative phrase "Riddled with light," which seems to invite the application of all the meanings of the word "riddle": *mystified* or *misled* with the vision, *explained* or *interpreted* with it, *punctured* with it, or even *corrupted*. (Unterecker, unaccountably misreading the line as "Riddled *by* light," also suggests that light's "shining conundrums" plague the poet.[13]) If the visionary poet assumes "all the blame out of all sense and reason," perhaps the vision has misled him. Possibly this one is an unreliable vision, a mis-

12 Unterecker, *A Reader's Guide*, 128.
13 *Ibid.*

taken insight, a punitive and malevolent inspiration which would unfairly burden him with a guilt that is not his. Even in the writing of *A Vision*, Yeats complains of the perplexing "Frustrators," who assumed the voices of his spiritual communicators but fed him misleading information which later had to be destroyed.

If this reading is defensible, it may seem to reduce the impact of the large question at the end of the poem: Is the ghost punished by the unjust skies? The question does not diminish in light of this reading, for it records profound doubt: even after death, does the injustice of this life persist? The poet who has so optimistically looked toward eventual harmony and reconciliation experiences a moment of indecision about whether life after death is really different and better. The "injustice of the skies" clearly postulates other than a benevolently controlled universe.

It is important to note that Yeats carefully avoids insisting upon the physical reality of the visionary image. It only *seemed* as though ice burned; the real vision is *inward*, just as the closing poem of the volume insists that it must be. And at the end of this poem he only *wonders* what the fate of his ghost may be, rather than stating its fate as predictable fact. Ellmann interprets such qualifications as uncertainty,[14] as they may well be; but their effect is to make the vision more powerfully convincing than it might have seemed had we been asked to believe that the sky actually contained burning ice, or that the ghost *would* be punished unjustly by the skies. Here as elsewhere, Yeats's ability to stand apart from an intense experience, even while presenting that experience in all its power and vividness, strengthens the total effect.

"The Magi," the second important visionary poem, would seem to belong among the *Vision*-related poems which Yeats began writing in 1917; it is surprising to observe how closely this poem, written in 1913, resembles those later ones in both theme and

14 Ellmann, *Yeats: The Man and the Masks,* 204.

image. Itself a visionary revelation, the poem suggests the recurrent cycles of history that would one day be examined and explained in the "Dove or Swan" section of *A Vision*. And the image of the Magi's appearing and disappearing in the sky as they seek fulfillment closely approximates the unending shuttle of the primary and antithetical gyres, waxing and waning but never attaining fulfillment.

The Magi, appearing to the poet "in the mind's eye," seek a repetition of the miracle at Bethlehem, "Being by Calvary's turbulence unsatisfied." But the poem is not confined to pointing out the limitation of Christianity; the Magi's appearing and disappearing "Now as at all times" indicates cyclic recurrence, suggesting that just as Christianity did not bring fulfillment, neither will the epoch which follows; nor did any epoch which preceded. Comparing their faces to "rain-beaten stones," Yeats emphasizes their timeless and fanatical persistence, for in his poetry a stone almost always symbolizes stubborn resistance to change; and a stone's erosion by water may require decades or even centuries. That these men are eternal questers, antedating as well as surviving by centuries the time of Christ, is perhaps reinforced by their not being called Magi in the poem itself; rather, they are "the pale unsatisfied ones," archetypal and timeless.

Here vision does not bring a solution but rather insight into the nature of conflict: there *is* no solution, but only perpetual struggle toward one. Since this idea is more fully discussed in the following chapter as the principal idea of *A Vision*, it must suffice at this point to indicate that "The Magi" anticipates by over four years that ambitious formulation.

The purpose of these visions goes far toward defining Yeats's conception of his role as an artist. As Grossman, among others, has pointed out, the sense in which Yeats's poet is a "daemonic man" is undoubtedly that of Plato's *Symposium*: "Everything that is daemonic is intermediate between god and mortal. Interpreting and conveying the wishes of man to gods and the will of gods to men, it stands between the two and fills the gap. . . . God has no contact with man; only through the daemonic is there intercourse and conversation between man and gods whether in the waking state or during sleep. And the man who is expert in such intercourse is the daemonic man."[15] A main current in RESPONSIBILITIES is this sense of a presence of hidden wisdom, or of one man's possessing insight that other men need but decline to accept. "To a Wealthy Man . . .," for example, lambasts its subject for failing to give freely that which "some day may breed the best," just as in "To a Shade" Parnell is told of the man (Lane) who could have given the Irish people that which "Had given their children's children loftier thought / Sweeter emotion." Other examples are "The Three Beggars," discussed above, and "The Mountain Tomb," in which Father Rosicross' body is miraculously preserved even though his secret wisdom remains "shut into his onyx eyes."

The volume emphasizes the importance of the past, visionary revelation, and art; and though Yeats recognizes and acknowledges the limitations of each of these, all of them will remain essential components of his quest, as demonstrated in the *Vision* poems discussed in the following chapter. Even if this volume reflects many forms of uncertainties, as so many observers claim, at least Yeats is continuing to establish and respect his own private traditions which—though imperfect in their way—need no longer be doubted.

15 Allen R. Grossman, *Poetic Knowledge in the Early Yeats: A Study of "The Wind Among the Reeds"* (Charlottesville: University Press of Virginia, 1969), 84.

6

The Early Vision Poems: Culmination of the Quest

FOUR DAYS after Yeats's marriage to George Hyde-Lees in October, 1917, his bride began to experiment with automatic writing in an attempt to distract Yeats from an unhappy state of mind. To their mutual astonishment strange sentences began to flow from Mrs. Yeats's hand; and Yeats promptly found himself engrossed in an enterprise that was to occupy him for almost the rest of his life. For over three years he transcribed almost daily communications from the spiritual advisors; then he labored over the task of arranging their revelations into a coherent literary form, culminating in the 1925 publication of *A Vision*; beyond that, he heavily revised and expanded the book, which was published in its final form in the autumn of 1937, scarcely more than a year before Yeats's death.

The product of twenty years of heavy labor and hard thought, *A Vision* has caused more critical anguish than any one of Yeats's poems. On one hand there has been enthusiastic agreement that no poet since Blake has made so ambitious an effort to create a personal myth as Yeats in *A Vision*; on the other hand, once the magnitude of the effort has been applauded, many critics have

137

turned away from *A Vision* in embarrassment or even annoyance because of the book's eccentric amalgamation of theosophy, spiritualism, Rosicrucianism, and neo-Platonism. Certainly Yeats made it no easier for his readers when he insisted, in the introduction to the revised version, that the entire system of *A Vision* had been communicated to him from the spirit world and that his own wife had served as medium.

When the book was first made available to the general public in the revised version, one of the kindest reviewers—Cecil Salkeld—offered reasons why the book could not even be treated "critically." [1] In 1931 Edmund Wilson undercut his otherwise generous praise of Yeats by accusing him of a dreamer's escapism; Wilson seemed to regret the very existence of *A Vision*: "If the whole thing . . . has been merely an invented mythology, in which Yeats himself does not believe, what right has he to bore us with it?" [2] Three years later J. Middleton Murry complained that Yeats had failed to submit his "idle dreaming" to the transforming power of creative energy.[3] In 1936, R. P. Blackmur contended that Yeats was essentially a poet of magic and that magic has "radical defects as a tool for poetry." [4] When Allen Tate countered these views in 1942, he evaded the issue somewhat by claiming that the system is not a mythology anyway, but an extended metaphor—thereby contradicting Yeats (who called it a personal mythology) in order to defend him.[5] Since then the troublesome scheme of *A Vision*—with its esoteric "system," eclectic symbolism, and rather bewildering diagrams and charts—has continued to be a major crux in Yeatsian criticism; as late as 1960 Yvor Winters issued a pamphlet in which Yeats's whole system is denounced as

1 Joseph Hone, *W. B. Yeats* (New York: Macmillan, 1943), 495.
2 Edmund Wilson, "W. B. Yeats," in James Hall and Martin Steinmann (eds.), *The Permanence of Yeats* (New York: Macmillan, 1961), 32.
3 J. Middleton Murry, "Mr. Yeats's Swan Song," *ibid.*, 10.
4 R. P. Blackmur, "The Later Poetry of W. B. Yeats," *ibid.*, 46.
5 Allen Tate, "Yeats's Romanticism: Notes and Suggestions," *ibid.*, 103.

"ridiculous," [6] and in which Yeats as a poet fares scarcely better. Others, like A. G. Stock, have been more charitable and have treated the book with the seriousness it deserves.[7] Whatever their private judgments of its merits may have been, almost all modern critics agree that *A Vision* illuminates much of Yeats's poetry, especially the later volumes.

Yeats's supernatural communicators promised him that their dictations, which came to be *A Vision*, would supply him with "metaphors for poetry." Indeed they did, and important metaphors at that; but beyond this contribution, *A Vision* imparts to the poetry, and contains within itself, Yeats's most noble and comprehensive formulation of a principle of universal order. The system is noble because Yeats manages to set aside his private stock of social, artistic, and intellectual preferences in order to devise a point of balance between all opposing forces: democratic and aristocratic, action and contemplation, the real and the ideal, day and night, life and death, and all others. The system is comprehensive not only because it balances all conceivable opposites, but also because it attempts to represent the dynamics of all human thought, all action, all historical movements, and all universal motion of which man can conceive, both in and out of time and space.

Here, finally, is a means of reconciling the antinomies—not by turning aside from human activity, as Yeats had been tempted to do as a younger man, in order to escape the opposing forces; not by calling down the apocalypse to burn away all creation so that a new and better world may blossom from its ashes; not by shouting down the opposition and apotheosizing one's own favorites. Rather, reconciliation is sought by accepting the principle of eternal conflict as a necessary fact of existence. "Without Con-

6 Yvor Winters, *The Poetry of W. B. Yeats,* Swallow Pamphlets, No. 10 (Denver, Colo., 1960).
7 See A. G. Stock, *W. B. Yeats: His Poetry and Thought* (Cambridge, Eng.:Cambridge University Press, 1961).

traries is no progression," Blake wrote in *The Marriage of Heaven and Hell*; Yeats in *A Vision* maintains that without contraries there is nothing at all: "All things are from antithesis, all things dying each other's life, living each other's death."

According to this theory, everything that exists—every idea, personality, or historical movement, for example—is at once half-created and half-qualified by its own opposite. The temper of each historical epoch is determined by that of the preceding epoch, which is its opposite. Hence, Yeats sees all action in quasi-Hegelian terms that closely suggest thesis, antithesis, and eventual synthesis. But although Yeats seems to perceive, like Hegel, a certain kind of progress in his system, so that every third action is not merely a repetition of the first, the symbolic framework which represents the system does not express progress. In seeking a symbol which can express every conceivable form of conflict, Yeats settles upon intersecting cones. Each half of the pair of opposites constitutes one cone, and it moves toward fulfillment (*i.e.,* expansion) by pushing against the other cone in the motion of a whirling gyre. As one cone comes as close to fulfillment as possible, it begins to be reduced by the push of the other cone in the opposite direction. These opposing cones, alternately waxing and waning, Yeats labels the *primary* and the *antithetical*.

Perceiving various correspondences somewhat in the manner of Baudelaire, Yeats establishes at various points in *A Vision* an accumulation of primary forces and antithetical forces: [8]

Primary	*Antithetical*
objective	subjective
space	time
democratic	aristocratic
externality	internality
reasonable	emotional/natural

8 The following list is my own deduction from Yeats's random statements throughout *A Vision* (Rev. ed.; New York: Macmillan, 1937.)

moral	aesthetic
solar	lunar
service	self-expression
enforced	free
code	personality
intellectually violent	personally violent
personally gentle	intellectually gentle
ugliness	beauty
dogmatic	expressive
leveling	hierarchical
unifying	multiple
feminine	masculine
humane	harsh
peaceful	surgical

If the primary and the antithetical are perfectly balanced within the interlocking gyres, each exerting equal pressure upon the other, the reader of *A Vision* would justifiably expect to find no preferential slant in either direction. But this is not the case. From the first, despite Yeats's admirable attempt to be fair to both sides, the antithetical has the better of the argument, not only as Yeats's own favored side, but as the perspective from which the whole system is examined and explained. In a sense Yeats seeks his own justification in making it plain from the start that *A Vision* is not a verbatim transcription of the supernatural dictations, but rather his own literary expression of the strange truths which were bestowed upon him. Yeats, with his lifelong devotion to the aesthetic principle, his distrust of the coldly rational, and his espousal of the aristocratic tradition, could hardly fall elsewhere than in the antithetical camp.

All looks yellow to the jaundiced eye, and the interesting thing about Yeats's antithetical bias is that it seems to be shared to some extent by his spiritual "instructors." Assuming that the correspondences listed above are the contribution of the instructors rather than Yeats's deductions based upon their basic information, we may question the fairness of their associating beauty with the antithetical and ugliness with the primary. It might have been more fair to associate, for instance, "the beauty of art" with the antithetical and "the beauty of scientific fact" with the primary, thereby admitting the possibility that to the primary man, primary forces may have their own beauty. Yet we are told, plainly and simply, that ugliness is characteristic of primary phases.

Terminology, too, favors the antithetical side of the balance. There are twenty-eight incarnations (or, more strictly, twenty-six incarnations and two of what Yeats calls "supernatural incarnations") through which the individual soul must pass in its twelve cycles of existence. These include an equal number of primary-dominant and antithetical-dominant incarnations; but all are described as *lunar* (hence, antithetical) phases, and Phase 1 is described as "absence of moon" rather than as the full presence of sun. It is amusing to imagine the protests that a primary man might voice against such an indication of bias.

If terminology is a minor indication, the goal of the human soul as it progresses through its various incarnations is a more significant instance of antithetical bias. As the soul makes its way through the twelve rounds of twenty-eight phases, its goal is apparently to gain an eventual synthesis of all human experience; in always pursuing one's mask or opposite, one seeks a wider, more comprehensive human experience. "Life," Yeats writes, "is an endeavour, made vain by the four sails of its mill, to come to a double contemplation, that of the chosen Image, that of the fated Image." [9] If the soul fails at any juncture to absorb all the experience that is possible within a particular incarnation, then it must repeat that phase before it can proceed to the next. It is fair, I think, to label the quest for wholeness an essentially antithetical

9 See Yeats, *A Vision*, 94.

one; its focus is upon the completion of selfhood rather than the primary subjection of the self's energies to something beyond. Hence the whole purpose of human life is seen as antithetical in nature.

Antithetical bias, no matter what form it takes in the chapters of *A Vision*, cannot obscure the essential fair-mindedness with which Yeats seeks to examine and to explain the unending interplay of opposite forces. In fact, in examining the evidence of bias, one is likely to marvel that a man so strong-willed and full of fight as Yeats, a man who had opposed the primary elements of his national culture in every conceivable public and private role, could concede to the enemy a full 50 percent portion of the universe. The venomous poet who sneered at the money-grubbing Paudeens, who denounced his country as a "fool-driven land," never intrudes upon the careful and beautiful balance of the *Vision* system, despite the subtle presence of antithetical bias throughout the volume.

The title indicates the essential modesty with which Yeats set about this most ambitious formulation of universal principles. *A* vision is not the same as *the* vision; it is but one of many possible ways of arranging the complexities of human experience and the universal design. It is an earnest, certainly ambitious, but always hypothetical schematization. When asked once why *A Vision* was so called, Yeats simply replied, "I am not permitted to tell." Possibly he meant that his spiritual communicators forbade him, or perhaps—as Hone suggests—the remark is an instance of his "humorous self-dramatization." [10] On the other hand, maybe he dismissed the question so lightly because he did not choose to defend or explain such a perfectly apt and revealing title.

As *a* vision, the book does not have to represent a literal conception of reality. Our belief in the system is neither requested nor

10 Hone, *W. B. Yeats*, 384.

required; the system is, as Cleanth Brooks says, "imaginatively true," [11] and that is enough. Yeats himself deals with this question in his introduction to the revised edition, in which he compares the system to the stylized techniques of modern art:

> Some will ask whether I believe in the actual existence of my circuits of sun and moon. . . . I can but answer that if sometimes, overwhelmed by miracle as all men must be when in the midst of it, I have taken such periods literally, my reason has soon recovered; and now that the system stands out clearly in my imagination I regard them as stylistic arrangements of experience comparable to the cubes in the drawing of Wyndham Lewis and to the ovoids in the sculpture of Brancusi. They have helped me to hold in a single thought reality and justice. [12]

The final phrase, "reality and justice" is particularly revealing. The system is intended to help the poet reconcile the chaotic real world with the ideal world of his own imagination—to impose (or, as he would prefer, to discern) a pattern. In this way the system is far more than a private mythology; it is an imaginative effort to frame an orderly cosmos. Here is the core of the reconciliation theme of the *Vision*-related poems.

It is difficult to select a group of poems which may be said to reflect the system of *A Vision* more than others, for the major symbols and certainly the major themes of the system had been germinating in Yeats's mind since the beginning of his career, as seen in some of the CROSSWAYS poems. But in the period extending from October, 1917 (when Mrs. Yeats's automatic writing began) through 1925 (the book's original publication date), Yeats published two volumes of poems, *The Wild Swans at Coole* in 1919 and *Michael Robartes and the Dancer* in 1921. Since these volumes were prepared during the time when Yeats was most absorbed in the formulation of the essential *Vision* system, they

11 Cleanth Brooks, Jr., "Yeats: The Poet as Myth-Maker," in Hall and Steinmann (eds.), *The Permanence of Yeats*, 84.
12 Yeats, *A Vision*, 24–25.

reflect more than earlier or later poems the tension and excitement of discovering a means of reconciling the real world and his own imaginative ideal.

Fortunately, most of the *Vision* poems are not mere versifications of the *Vision* system; the gyres, moon phases, and other images have undergone a poetic transformation so that, in most cases, they serve the poem rather than govern it. When the poetry is read in relation to *A Vision*'s formal system, each poem must ultimately stand on its own, apart from any or all of its sources. Balachandra Rajan's warning in this regard seems appropriate: "The danger of reading Yeats's poetry as *A Vision* versified is that the excellence of the poetry tends to depend on the efficiency with which *A Vision* is rendered. Once this criterion is abandoned, as it should be, then the alternative must be that the poem establishes and justifies itself." [13]

Yeats closes the RESPONSIBILITIES volume with a somewhat embittered resolution to rid his verse of "embroideries / Out of old mythologies," for he concludes that "there's more enterprise / In walking naked." It is characteristic of Yeats, whose image-rich poetry never walked naked, that the first poem of the next volume, the title poem of THE WILD SWANS AT COOLE, already anticipates the embroidery of the *new* mythology, which will be that of *A Vision*.

"The Wild Swans at Coole," after reflecting the poet's lament against old age and loss of passion, asks the ambitious question that *A Vision* will offer an answer to: what is the relation between this world and that one beyond death? Though the final lines express Yeats's assumption that there really is life after death ("when I awake some day"), the poem formulates no answer to this question; it awaits an answer from the poems that follow. Nevertheless, the imagery of this poem anticipates the machinery with which Yeats will eventually formulate a reconciliation of the

13 Balachandra Rajan, *W. B. Yeats: A Critical Introduction* (London: Hutchinson University Library, 1965), 92.

two worlds: the interacting gyres. Many have observed the gyre-like formation of the wild swans as they "suddenly mount / And scatter wheeling in great broken rings." This formation makes the central image of *A Vision* available to the visionary quester who stands there before the swans, but he is not yet able to recognize that image. Hence the swans' formation may function in much the same way as the circling formation of the bat in the later poem, "The Phases of the Moon." Whereas the man who stands before the swans perceives no answer to his question, the quester in the tower suddenly perceives in the circling of the bat the key to visionary understanding, as signified by his abruptly putting out the lamp in his tower.

It is ironic that one might confront such an image and remain unaware of its mystic significance; it is even more ironic that the speaker in "The Wild Swans at Coole" has retained the image in his memory for almost two decades and yet remains blind to its potential. (Since the title poem was written before Yeats's marriage, this irony could not, of course, have been deliberate if one accepts Yeats's claim that he gained the image of the gyres from his spiritual advisors. In any case, his later placement of the poem in this key position in the volume may suggest that he was by then alert to the irony.) For the swans do not gyre upward in the present time of the poem; the speaker only recalls their doing so nineteen years earlier when he first set out to count them.

Of course, even if he were able to seize upon the gyre image and fully realize its symbolic potential, a great deal more visionary insight must arrive before he could formulate a reconciliation of the worlds of the living and of the dead. The whole mood of the poem is one of incompleteness, or more specifically, of *near-completeness*. The speaker's life has moved a long distance toward completeness since he first saw the swans, but he longs to know something of what awaits him after death; even a completed lifetime is not complete, but is resumed beyond the grave. The swans wheeled in "great *broken* rings" (italics mine). The trees "are in their autumn beauty," their life cycle not yet complete; the month is October—the incompleted year; the nearly ended day is at twilight (presumably evening, in this case). It can even be argued that the swans, for all their seeming immortality, are not complete, since there are only fifty-nine of them, not sixty—a fact one is apt to recall when in the fourth stanza the swans swim and climb the air "lover by lover." One swan, at least, lacks a lover.[14]

Of course, maybe there were only fifty-nine swans at Coole Park, and in fact nineteen years had passed since Yeats had first seen them. But the poetic application of these incomplete odd numbers, both of them so close to fulfillment of a decade, suggests something more than literal description. It suggests, perhaps, that fulfillment is near at hand, that the poems to follow will round out visionary wisdom and answer the brooding question of the closing lines of the poem.

The ending seems optimistic in tone as it poses this question. In fact, Yeats made it more so in the process of revision. In an intermediate draft he had written "when I come here some day" instead of the original and final "when I awake some day." The final version is infinitely richer; it suggests not only that renewed life awaits man beyond the grave, but also that it may be a heightened form of life, in comparison to which mere earthly life is only an extended sleep or maybe a dream.

There are many to whom the whole poem as well as the closing lines seem far less optimistic, of course. Bloom and Jeffares conclude that the poem's dominant emotion is the poet's sorrow that his passion for Maud Gonne has waned.[15] Having felt depressed nineteen years earlier when Maud Gonne first declined his marriage proposal, Yeats—according to Bloom—now feels depressed

---

14 Robert W. Caswell has commented on this detail in his article, "Yeats's Odd Swan at Coole," *Eire*, 4, ii (1969), 81–86.
15 Harold Bloom, *Yeats* (New York: Oxford University Press, 1970), 192; Norman Jeffares, *W. B. Yeats: Man and Poet* (2nd ed.; New York: Barnes and Noble, 1966), 222.

"for *not* feeling depression at the continued refusal." Even if his continuing frustration over Maud Gonne were on his mind as Yeats composed the poem, Bloom's reading seems to me to restrict the poem quite unnecessarily by overstressing the biographical element, especially since the poet laments the condition of heart-weariness without even a veiled allusion to Maud Gonne. Whatever may have inspired the poem, it is *about* the universal facts of waning passion, old age, and death, and not about the poet's passion for Maud Gonne.

But it is with Bloom's reading of the final stanza that my own most sharply differs. He reads the clause "when I awake some day" to signify, not death, and certainly not life after death, but rather "the end of *antithetical* consciousness, the complete breaking with the Shelleyan influence."[16] Shelley aside, this reading is at first tempting: since the whole poem laments the loss of passion, the final stanza might logically seem to lament the regrettable necessity for awakening from the beautiful antithetical dream into the harsh primary world of old age and death. One problem with this reading is that the poet has already experienced heart-weariness and loss of passion, yet has not awakened from the antithetical dream. If it has not happened yet, when is it to happen? What further event is to signal his complete break from the antithetical? Since Bloom does not allow Ellmann's reading of "awake" to mean death,[17] one is left to puzzle over how Bloom would explain the "some day."

Another problem is that "The Wild Swans at Coole" introduces a volume of poems in which the antithetical attitude is vigorously upheld at the expense of the primary attitude. Age and the supposed waning of passion notwithstanding, Yeats is more solidly wedded to the antithetical dream in this volume than ever before.

16 Bloom, *Yeats*, 193.
17 Bloom refers to Richard Ellmann, *The Identity of Yeats* (New York: Oxford University Press, 1964), 253, although he slightly misquotes the passage.

Why, then, would he place a poem falsely prophesying the loss of antithetical consciousness at the head of a large group of antithetically governed poems? Bloom himself concedes that "the prophecy was not fulfilled, perhaps because such an awakening would have been a death-in-life for Yeats, even after love was dead." Does this mean that the poet had the freedom to choose whether to abandon his antithetical commitment? Presumably he had no such choice, or he would have had no cause to lament old age and loss of passion in the first place.

Those who do not share my feeling that the final lines are optimistic gain points for their argument from Yeats's original arrangement of the stanzas. He originally placed the final stanza in the middle of the poem, so that the poem ended with what is now the penultimate stanza, which ends: "Passion or conquest, wander where they will, / Attend upon them still." Admittedly, if the poem closed with this reflection upon the swans' lasting passion, as opposed to man's waning passion, the effect would certainly not be optimistic. But Yeats repositioned the stanzas in order to achieve a greatly different effect at the end. Perhaps he intended the note of optimism, looking far ahead to some idyllic future time, as he so often does in his poetry; or perhaps he enjoyed the ambiguous effect of the word "awake," which, though it may confound Yeats's critics, may delight his less combative readers with its double-edged possibilities.

In the poem "On Woman," Yeats again reflects upon the loss of passion in old age; and in this case no one is likely to deny that he hopefully anticipates renewal of passion in an afterlife beyond the grave. Having reviewed the rich pleasures that woman brings to man, he starts to ask God for a woman's hand (or, as seems more likely in this case, her body) then draws back:

> For I am not so bold
> To hope a thing so dear
> Now I am growing old,
> But when, if the tale's true,

> The Pestle of the moon
> That pounds up all anew
> Brings me to birth again—
> To find what once I had
> And know what once I have known,
> Until I am driven mad,
> Sleep driven from my bed,
> By tenderness and care

Since "the tale" concerning the life-renewing "Pestle of the moon" must surely be the evolving revelation of *A Vision*, Yeats is unlikely to be skeptical of what it predicts. The only sour note in this optimistic anticipation is the tenth line quoted above: "Until I am driven mad." It would be too easy to read this line as an example of trivial hyperbole of the pop-music variety ("mad with passion," "mad with desire") even though the apparent meaning of the line in context invites such a reading. Yeats is especially fond of planting inconspicuous qualifiers in the midst of a seemingly innocent assertion, as he does in poems as dissimilar as "In the Seven Woods" and "Sailing to Byzantium." Here the close association of madness with the poet's dream of a sensually pleasurable afterlife ought to be noted carefully: maybe it is mere hyperbole, and maybe it is a caution that the imagination has a perilous, even destructive aspect.

If I seem to be overly concerned with this superficially innocuous line, the poem "Broken Dreams" may justify my caution. The poet, stung by his memories of a woman's beauty, reassures himself: "But in the grave all, all, shall be renewed." At first this seems simply another example of Yeats's confidence in an afterlife; but the stanza continues thus:

> The certainty that I shall see that lady
> Leaning or standing or walking
> In the first loveliness of womanhood,
> And with the fervour of my youthful eyes,
> Has set me muttering like a fool.

The two poems are alike in linking dreams of the afterlife with madness; the first poem pictures madness occurring in the afterlife, but the second poem shows it occurring much earlier—the poet "muttering like a fool" because of his imaginative certainty that a new life will restore youth. (The context of the second poem assures us that this "fool" is not the blessed Fool of the *Vision* system; if he were, it would be a compliment to "mutter like a fool.") Yeats seems to worry that his conviction in the afterlife may be ill-placed.

The title character of "Tom O'Roughley," who has much in common with the *Vision* Fool, voices still another certainty in an afterlife; and this time there is no obvious association with madness: "What's dying but a second wind?" So far as one can judge, Tom—unlike the aging poet—has no particular personal reason to long for the afterlife; but so confident is he of this "second wind" that he concludes: "And if my dearest friend were dead / I'd dance a measure on his grave." Tom, who has attained the irrational joy that Yeats so warmly applauds, voices Yeats's own attitude in scorning the "logic-choppers" and approving "aimless joy." But often Yeats seems not so much to share as to *wish* to share the vigorous confidence and joyous simplicity of his peasant characters; possibly Tom voices an easy confidence in the afterlife, which Yeats would like to feel if he were not bound to the inescapable complexities and ambiguities of his own intellect. In the early poems Yeats could not opt for the world of dreams at the expense of the world of reality; here, too, he is swayed simultaneously toward idyllic dreams of the afterlife and the more practical world where such dreaming seems mere foolishness. As in the interacting gyres, when one pushes the antithetical dream to its ultimate, the dream begins to wane and the force of primary reality begins to make itself felt.

Here as elsewhere the tension between antinomial forces lends power to Yeats's poetry and dignity to his intellectual position; for he remains loyal to the experiential realm even when he would choose to embrace a life beyond experience. As always before, Yeats seeks reconciliation of opposites, not the elimination of options.

Yeats's imaginative hope for reincarnation, even when it is qualified by the reservations discussed above, functions as a potent shield against the primary culture in these poems. His confidence in a new life in which present wrongs will at last be remedied enables him to embrace the antithetical life without despair, defensiveness, or even his usual brand of anger at the primary environment. The point of view of the poems in THE WILD SWANS AT COOLE well demonstrates his achievement of a mature vision; in many of the poems he looks toward what he would like to be—wild, exultant, free, passionate, "Ignorant and wanton as the dawn"—and in many others he looks backward at his youth and laments the losses that accompany advancing age. What gives these poems much of their power (and no previous volume excelled this one) is his vantage point somewhere past youth and short of old age. When he laments his loss of passion, we are deeply moved by his eloquence and sincerity; but ironically, there is more emotional power manifested in these laments than in most of the poems he had written as a much younger man.

Here Yeats, moving rapidly toward ultimate acceptance of conflict through the design of *A Vision*, is markedly less vicious in his denunciation of the primary world around him. In "The People," Maud Gonne points out to him that even when the crowds reviled her, she never complained of them; the poet seeks to defend his own complaints against them by showing that he and she are opposite personalities:

> All I could reply
> Was: 'You, that have not lived in thought but deed,
> Can have the purity of a natural force,
> But I, whose virtues are the definitions
> Of the analytic mind, can neither close
> The eye of the mind nor keep my tongue from speech.'

He concludes the poem, however, with the admission that he was abashed by her words—that even nine years after she uttered them, he remains abashed. Certainly he is no fonder of the primary culture, but he seems to see it more and more as part of an overall design which is impervious to his verbal assaults. In place of angry satire, he seems to write these poems out of an assumption that since the world mood is beyond his control, a man of his own antithetical temperament has no defense against it other than turning his back to it and working toward a mood of private exultation. Nowhere is this exultation better achieved than in "An Irish Airman Foresees His Death," in which Robert Gregory, indifferent to the political cross-purposes of the turbulent primary world, chooses to follow, even to his own death, "A lonely impulse of delight":

> I balanced all, brought all to mind,
> The years to come seemed waste of breath,
> A waste of breath the years behind
> In balance with this life, this death.

Of the several spokesmen who follow, or wish to follow, antithetical impulses of delight, only Gregory receives a solemn treatment, probably because this poem is in a sense an elegiac comment. The others would escape the stultifying primary world through a joyous, oblivious primitivism such as that of "Tom O'Roughley":

> 'An aimless joy is a pure joy,'
> .   .   .   .
> 'And wisdom is a butterfly
> And not a gloomy bird of prey.'

Or that of the poet himself, expressed thus in "The Dawn":

> I would be—for no knowledge is worth a straw—
> Ignorant and wanton as the dawn.

In "The Collar-Bone of a Hare" the sought-after primitivism assumes the familiar form of an idyllic, faraway island of music and dancing, one which is essentially the same island as that to which Oisin was transported (*The Wanderings of Oisin*) and on which the hapless CROSSWAYS lovers vainly sought immortal passion ("The Indian to His Love"). A comparison of "The Collar-Bone of a Hare" with the CROSSWAYS poem demonstrates an essential difference between the antithetical idylls of the younger and the older Yeats, a difference which might easily be overlooked if the later poem were read only within the context of THE WILD SWANS AT COOLE.

This difference is that the later poem, vastly more vigorous and comprehensive, indicates a partial reconciliation of the opposing worlds of the antithetical dream-ideal and the primary reality. The CROSSWAYS poem evokes a muted, static atmosphere where the escapist lovers murmur "how far away are the unquiet lands," and this murmur is the only intrusion of the real world upon their idyll until the final lines of the poem suggest (as explained in the first chapter) that their bliss may not endure forever after all. The later poem, in contrast, describes an island of lively music and dance, a place populated by many kings, kings' daughters, and dancing partners, unlike the lonely CROSSWAYS isle where the only other inhabitants appear to be peahens, parrots, and doves. The dreamer in the later poem would not merely hide on the island, as the lover did ("Hid under quiet boughs apart"); he would learn for himself the lesson of antithetical joy and ease, apart from "the old bitter world where they marry in churches." In the earlier poem the "unquiet lands" remain far away, but in the later one the dreamer will turn again toward the real world and "laugh over the untroubled water / At all who marry in churches." There is no such laughter, or anything like it, in the earlier poem.

In short, Yeats laments the impossibility of dream-escape in the first poem; in the second, he does not so much escape as barricade himself to prepare for confrontation. In earlier poetry he had to remind himself that one must finally face the enemy; here he confidently welcomes that event. Only in full maturity can Yeats laugh across the wide gulf that divides the primary and the antithetical realms.

Much closer to the machinery of *A Vision* is the primitivism of "Solomon to Sheba," in which the two lovers conclude after a half-day of discussion that "There's not a thing but love can make / The world a narrow pound." Each of the three stanzas refers to the progression from midday to night, symbolically suggesting Phase 1 of the ultimate primary dominance (full sun) through Phase 15 of the ultimate antithetical dominance (full moon). Their having "gone round and round" seems to be a clear allusion to the motion of the gyres; and the references to their lovemaking, which occur in the second line of each of the three stanzas, suggest that their final discovery has come about not through intellectual disputation but rather through joyous sexuality. And, significantly, the revelation comes in the antithetical night. The three oppositions—male/female, day/night, and reason/instinct—are reconciled through the power of love, and the reconciliation itself is an antithetical triumph.

Although it is a dangerous undertaking to attempt to discover patterns in Yeats's arrangement of his poems within a volume, especially in so large and varied a collection as THE WILD SWANS AT COOLE, it is nonetheless interesting that Yeats intersperses the passionate, optimistic, antithetically joyous poems among the laments at loss of passion and youth. This arrangement, deliberate or not, increases the reader's consciousness of the conflict of opposite viewpoints and sharpens the urgency of reconciliation. For example, after the antithetical joy in the face of death expressed in "An Irish Airman Foresees His Death" comes the gloomy "Men Improve with the Years," which ends:

> But I grow old among dreams,
> A weather-worn, marble triton
> Among the streams.

Immediately following this despairing note is "The Collar-Bone of a Hare," celebrating the antithetical with music and dance and laughter. After the joyous antithetical discovery of "Solomon to Sheba" come two laments, "The Living Beauty":

> O heart, we are old;
> The living beauty is for younger men:
> We cannot pay its tribute of wild tears.

and "A Song":

> *For who could have foretold*
> *That the heart grows old?*

But immediately after these comes "To a Young Beauty," in which the aging poet praises "the winters gone" and boasts that he "may dine at journey's end / With Landor and with Donne." This arrangement is in itself an indication of Yeats's ultimate acceptance of conflict and mutability, for it suggests that he means to temper the extremes of both optimism and depression by posing their opposites against them.

As if to announce his successful schematization of this inter-play of opposites, Yeats presents at the end of the volume a group of poems which specifically announce and seek to explicate *A Vision*'s complex treatment of opposites. After the sharply alter-nating moods of the previous poems, Yeats provides the clash of opposing attitudes in a single poem, "Ego Dominus Tuus," the first of the explicitly *Vision*-related group. The poem is cast in the form of a dialogue between *Hic*, who represents primary man, and *Ille*, who represents not just antithetical man but apparently Yeats himself. *Ille* paces the sands outside his "old wind-beaten tower, where still / A lamp burns on beside the open book / That Michael Robartes left," seeking revelation through the discovery of his antiself.

Already *A Vision* has made its entrance, for in the original edition of that book Yeats devises a fictional account of its origin which depends upon an ancient book in the possession of Michael

Robartes. Moreover, the antithetical *Ille* walks, significantly, "in the moon," and *Hic* identifies him with those aging, antithetical visionaries of earlier poems such as "Lines Written in Dejection" when he says, "you walk in the moon, / And, though you have passed the best of life, still trace, / Enthralled by the unconquerable delusion, / Magical shapes."

After considerable critical discussion it remains moot whether this poem succeeds as a poem or functions mainly as an explication of the *Vision* doctrine of the mask. As Bloom observes, its rich, rhetorical style is able to obscure that which, divorced from that style, would seem somewhat nonsensical—such as the treatment of Keats as "ignorant." [18] But apart from what style may conceal, the poem is heavily weighted in favor of the antithetical viewpoint of *Ille*. *Hic*'s presence seems required, in fact, only to serve as a springboard for *Ille*'s superior, antithetical ideas. This fact seems to me to rob the poem of much of its potential tension, and to impose an element of didacticism where even a mere explication of *A Vision* would, if conducted fairly, give additional force to the primary side of the balance.

Hic speaks twenty-six lines to *Ille's* fifty-nine; *Ille* get the final word; and, most important, the whole discussion focuses upon *Ille*'s own pursuit of his antiself. Hence the "debate," as it is often called, is a rather artificial one in which the winner has been established before the first words are spoken. Nor is the poem written as if Yeats were working out his ideas as it progresses; *Ille*'s first speech announces his firm position and his succeeding ones defend and explain that position with no wavering, no apparent struggle for affirmation or decision on either speaker's part. It is doubtless somewhat unfair to complain that a poem is not structured as one would like, but my point is simply that this poem seems to masquerade as a debate when in fact its purpose is to explain and defend Yeats's own doctrine of the mask; it does

18 Bloom, *Yeats*, 203.

not demonstrate the tensely balanced conflict of opposites which characterize his best *Vision* poems and *A Vision* itself.

Ille's opposition to the primary man of action ends in a curious comment upon the function and importance of art:

> For those that love the world serve it in action,
> Grow rich, popular and full of influence,
> And should they paint or write, still it is action:
> The struggle of the fly in marmalade.
> The rhetorician would deceive his neighbours,
> The sentimentalist himself; while art
> Is but a vision of reality.
> What portion in the world can the artist have
> Who has awakened from the common dream
> But dissipation and despair?

Art is but a vision of reality. On one level this statement suggests that the artist deals in truth, unlike the rhetorician and the sentimentalist, who deal in deception. On another level, however, art is *but* a *vision* of reality: perhaps it offers no reality but that of vision itself and hence is preoccupied with that which lies apart from any reality except its own form. What may seem, according to one reading, a bold defense of art as a revelation of reality threatens to become, by the other reading, a mere statement of preference for art that may express no reality but its own static form. Is the artist a visionary realist, then, or merely a visionary aesthete?

This problem, it seems to me, is more true to the complexity of Yeats's own vision and craft than anything else in the poem. As in "Easter 1916" and "Sailing to Byzantium" and many lesser but distinguished poems, the poet here toys with conflicting notions and manages to affirm both of them simultaneously. This, surely, is the kind of Yeatsian tension and energy which might transform "Ego Dominus Tuus" into a more compelling work of art if it were explored more fully than in this single line of the poem. As it stands, with *Hic* a mere sparring partner, the poem lacks true tension and offers little more than the eloquence of its doctrinal explication.

In the final speech of the poem *Ille* looks forward to the arrival of his antiself, the "mysterious one" who will whisper all the truths *Ille* seeks

> . . . as though
> He were afraid the birds, who cry aloud
> Their momentary cries before it is dawn,
> Would carry it away to blasphemous men.

His prophecy is fulfilled in "The Phases of the Moon." *Aherne, Ille's* almost diabolical antiself, suggests that his companion *Robartes* should reward the long-suffering poet in the tower with a mere morsel of the great truths he seeks, just enough to drive him insane with longing. *Robartes* then recites the characteristics of the lunar phases, truths of which the poet—high in his tower—remains unaware. Finally *Aherne* hisses a fragment of truth concerning the last three phases ("Hunchback and Saint and Fool . . . ") and a bat rises gyre-like in the air; the light in the tower is at last extinguished. The moment of revelation, long awaited, has finally arrived.

There are two possible sources for this revelation: either the poet has overheard the final words of *Aherne*, or he has perceived the significance of the image of the gyring bat. The latter possibility is more likely, not only because of the physical impossibility of *Aherne's* low voice being heard high up in the tower, but also because the poem seems to comment upon the *manner* of the poet's perception of truth—through image rather than through intellectual idea. The poet in his tower struggles toward the details which *Aherne* and *Robartes* already possess; but his light is put out when he perceives the gyre image, for that is the key that will unlock the rest, just as in *A Vision*.

The reader who cherishes Yeats's poetry above his philosophy (and, as with so many poets, the two are frequently at odds) may regret, as I do, that the whole poem does not profit from Yeats's expression of the poet's imagistic mode. "The Phases of the Moon" is a slack, dogmatic exercise, only occasionally enlivened by "poetic" moments, as if the poet were straining to poeticize a classroom lecture. The image of the gyre reaches the poet in the tower too late to make this particular poem successful.

As if to offer proof that the tower light was not extinguished prematurely, Yeats includes three poems which treat the extended subjects of that revelation: "The Saint and the Hunchback," "Two Songs of a Fool," and "Another Song of a Fool," all of which depend in varying degrees upon the system of *A Vision* for adequate comprehension. Before these comes "The Cat and the Moon," a poem which, though unmistakably a *Vision* poem, surpasses all the others in this group in its flawless fusion of *Vision* elements with the more crucially requisite element of felt and observed experience.

Though it is imbued with the *Vision* doctrine of inescapable earthly changes in response to the various lunar phases, "The Cat and the Moon" derives as directly from Yeats's sensitive appreciation of the ways of cats as from the self-willed mystical mood of the *Vision* poems. Minnaloushe is not merely a symbol of earthbound creatures who must change as the moon changes; he is not even *primarily* a symbol; he is a cat. The mood of the poem strikes me as deceptively playful, probably not nearly so "cheerful" as Unterecker views it.[19] Tempering the exhilaration that must naturally follow upon the moment of revelation recorded by the previous poem, this poem offers a brief, gentle, but essentially serious reminder of helplessness and impermanence beneath the ever-changing moon.

The cat Minnaloushe, "the nearest kin of the moon," represents the epitome of the antithetical personality. Troubled by the shining presence of his kinsman above him, he performs a kind

19 John Unterecker, *A Reader's Guide to William Butler Yeats* (New York: Noonday Press, 1959), 153.

of dance with the moon as the "sacred moon" gradually changes phase . The poem ends:

> Does Minnaloushe know that his pupils
> Will pass from change to change,
> And that from round to crescent,
> From crescent to round they range?
> Minnaloushe creeps through the grass
> Alone, important and wise,
> And lifts to the changing moon
> His changing eyes.

The question in this passage seems to require a whispered "no" in reply, for Minnaloushe, who only *seems* wise, knows nothing of the change even as his own eyes begin to change; his mystical bond with the moon troubles only his animal blood, not his consciousness. Hence the poem serves as a not-so-cheerful indication of mortal helplessness in face of the shifting gyres which govern man's being. The poem also raises the old question whether the only wisdom one can hope to achieve is knowledge of one's own helplessness. In the later poems, particularly those which deal with tragic joy, this consideration becomes increasingly important.

The final poem of the volume is "The Double Vision of Michael Robartes," a difficult symbolic representation of the two extreme lunar phases and the human life that must exist always between those extremes. In the final lines the speaker reflects upon his moment of vision:

> Thereon I made my moan,
> And after kissed a stone,
>
> And after that arranged it in a song,
> Seeing that I, ignorant for so long,
> Had been rewarded thus
> In Cormac's ruined house.

The permanence of song is contrasted here with the impermanence of the "ruined house," the site of revelation. The birth of the song within the decayed house suggests the double cones once again, living each other's death, dying each other's life. Thus Yeats expresses both his consciousness of inevitable decay and his conviction that the work of art may stand against the mutability of all the world, as if art (as a record of visionary revelation) were the only means of escape from the deterministic gyring of time and space. It is by now a familiar theme in his poetry, and one that is expressed with ever-increasing conviction.

MICHAEL ROBARTES AND THE DANCER, though it contains five of Yeats's finest poems (including the incomparable "The Second Coming" and "Easter 1916"), contributes surprisingly little to the development of the *Vision* system in his poetry. The usual themes are rather casually reiterated once or twice, and the complexities of moon phase and personality type seem momentarily suspended; the one aspect of *A Vision* which lends tension and urgency to several of these poems is Yeats's perennial consciousness of ambivalence. More here than ever before, he seems to enjoy toying with opposites, juxtaposing them without resolving their tension except by suggesting, as in the interlocking gyre image, that they are evenly matched.

An illustration of this ambivalence is "Solomon and the Witch," the first of five or six poems in this volume that can be called *Vision* poems. As Solomon and Sheba frolic "under the wild moon," Sheba cries out suddenly in a "strange tongue," and her wise lover informs her that the sound was that of a cockerel who has not crowed thus since just before the fall of man:

> And never crew again till now,
> And would not now but that he thought,
> Chance being at one with Choice at last,
> All that the brigand apple brought
> And this foul world were dead at last.
> He that crowed out eternity
> Thought to have crowed it in again.

The exuberant pronouncement of these same lovers in the previous volume, that only love could make "the world a narrow pound," is here amplified: lovemaking has almost united the contraries of Chance and Choice and brought about the end of the world of conflict—almost, but not quite. Bright with hope, the Arab lady ends the poem by addressing her lover thus: " 'And the moon is wilder every minute. / O! Solomon! let us try again.' "

At its most obvious level the poem displays the kind of antithetical fulfillment that Yeats most approved: Sheba and Solomon think with their bodies as well as their minds, and if the cockerel's cry is a valid indication, their body-thinking is nearly as effective as the other (for the previous poem informs us that they are the wisest among men). But the surface of the poem is deceptively joyous in tone. The title is the first indication of the presence of peril, for Sheba is a "witch." Her witchery is apparent in the spell she has cast over her lover as she blithely endeavors to bring about the end of the world, heedless of the terror of such an undertaking. This element of terror is reinforced by the implied parallel between these lovers and Adam and Eve; Sheba's whimsical urge to end the world repeats Eve's offering the apple and ending that earlier world.

Terror is implicit, too, in the prophetic cry of the cockerel, which suggests other wild bird cries in such poems as "Ego Dominus Tuus" and "The Phases of the Moon." These cries mingle an element of foreboding with that of revelation, as in the later poem, "The Second Coming." The fact that the cockerel's cry has presaged the fall of man, and is now expected to renew eternity, reveals the ambiguity of the image in this poem. Other hints that imply complexities beyond mere sensual bliss are the *forbidden* sacred grove in which the lovers lie and the moon which grows *wilder* every minute. Hence the lurking presence of terror undercuts antithetical joy even at the approach of the unearthly purity of Phase 15. For all her wisdom and antithetical strengths, Sheba toys with perilous structures.

A more dramatic use of ambivalence occurs throughout "Easter 1916," deservedly one of the most widely discussed of Yeats's poems. It would be merely repetitive to explore the ambivalent structure of the poem here, in view of the many excellent discussions already in print; in any case, one need only recall the poem's key line, "A terrible beauty is born," to appreciate the central ambivalence. What begins as a respectful acknowledgment of the sacrifice of Irish patriots in the Easter uprising of 1916 soon shifts to a nervous reflection upon the patriots' unyielding fanaticism ("Too long a sacrifice / Can make a stone of the heart."); and in the end Yeats leaves to heaven the task of judging these men. It is not that he dodges the issue; rather, the poem itself is his confrontation of the unwelcome possibility that their lives were hardened and then lost for no justifiable end. And Yeats—fully cognizant of the issues weighing upon both sides—simultaneously praises the patriotic sacrifice and regrets its fanatical rashness. Like children who sleep at last after their "limbs . . . had run wild," the dead patriots seem in retrospect both endearingly childlike and disturbingly childish. The poem is a beautiful reconciliation of the poet's opposing emotions, true to the positive and negative sides of the balance without arbitrarily forcing a conclusion.

"Demon and Beast" is no less ambiguous; but here the poet depends upon irony rather than direct statement to express the opposing views, and here one side seems to have the better of the argument. It is a poem that would be distressingly smug if one were to accept it at face value: the poet seems to turn aside from more serious considerations in order to congratulate himself that old age has at last delivered him from the demon and beast of "hatred and desire." Having apparently achieved the "aimless joy" he had sought for years (as described in the earlier poem "Tom O'Roughley"), he stops to watch a white gull:

> Now gyring down and perning there
> He splashed where an absurd
> Portly green-pated bird

> Shook off the water from his back;
> Being no more demoniac
> A stupid happy creature
> Could rouse my whole nature.

The poem is such a storehouse of self-congratulatory remarks that the serious reader is justified in suspecting the redeeming presence of irony. For one thing, the next poem in the volume— "The Second Coming" itself, no less—will again present the image of the bird assisting in a demoniac activity, the "indignant desert birds" whose shadows reel over the terrible creature that slouches toward Bethlehem. Such an image, following so closely upon this one, would seem to belie the poet's happy consideration that the white gull or green-pated bird is, after all, only a "stupid happy creature." The point may be that whether we are able to respond to the poetic image or perceive only the surface reality of the "stupid happy creature," the terrible realities which poetic images record are nonetheless realities, and they are no less terrible for our ignorance of them. If this is so, the speaker of "Demon and Beast" has momentarily deceived himself into believing only in the surface reality, the reality of what he sees with his eyes rather than what he has seen with his finer imagination.

Particularly suspect are the lines

> Yet I am certain as can be
> . . . .
> . . . that mere growing old, that brings
> Chilled blood, this sweetness brought;

More than once Yeats employs a doggerel phrase like "certain as can be" in his poetry, and each time the phrase seems meant to be taken both on its casual surface level and on a more serious, literal level: that is, in this instance being certain *as can be* means, not simply the ultimate degree of certainty, but the inability to be very certain at all. Moreover, in countless other poems Yeats strongly refutes the idea that the sweetness brought by old age is worth the price of chilled blood. Despite the poet's reflection upon "exultant Anthony" starved and withered to a bag of bones, the hideous and alarming visual image of that condition more than cancels the force of the word *exultant*. If the poet is reaching out for some form of transcendent gaiety, he is simultaneously horrified at the image of bodily ruin. The result seems somewhat muddled: Is Yeats suggesting, as he seems to be, that one must be content with his lot, with a spiritual insight into the inner nature of things? This strikes me as an unconvincing posture for Yeats, for it is a consolation belonging to men with "chilled blood"; worse still, it is a consolation of ascetics. Somehow Yeats must manage to have it both ways: the passion and the vision simultaneously. But Choice and Chance are not yet united and may never be; the conflict of opposites, poetically and actually, has not yet been resolved.

"The Second Coming," one of the greatest of the *Vision* poems, overwhelmingly refutes the complacency of the spokesman in "Demon and Beast": there is no escape from the demoniac. Because the gyre is ever-widening, things *must* eventually fall apart; "the centre cannot hold." He who was blind to the prophetic gyring of the white gull in "Demon and Beast" must be unprepared for the "rough beast" and the new era about to unfold. The future itself cannot be known; but the inevitability of violent, disruptive change can be known. "The Second Coming" offers *A Vision*'s cyclic account of history: there is a visionary reconciliation of opposites implicit in the large view of history which reveals a counterforce for every force, a victory for every defeat, a defeat for every victory. And though one may recoil from the "rough beast" that ushers in revolution, the poem reminds him that the gentle Child in the manger had Himself "vexed to nightmare" a long age of stony sleep.

In "The Second Coming," what is not known about the coming era far outweighs what is known, despite the visionary force of the images themselves. This acknowledgment of the vastness of the unknowable is characteristic of Yeats's poetry, especially at this phase of his career; even in a brief poem like "A Meditation in Time of War," the very essence of which is an assertion of what is suddenly perceived, the unknown and the unknowable are subtly acknowledged. At first the poem may seem more confidently assertive than it in fact is:

> For one throb of the artery,
> While on that old grey stone I sat
> Under the old wind-broken tree,
> I knew that One is animate,
> Mankind inanimate phantasy.

Unterecker says of the poem that it suggests "the prophet's consolation: he has seen into the essential pattern of all things. Reality is in the Platonic forms . . . ; mankind is the shadowy imitation, the 'inanimate phantasy,' of the grand design."[20] Although this is a satisfactory reading, I am troubled by the arrangement of the last two lines of the poem, which seem to offer a second reading: One is animate *phantasy* and mankind is inanimate phantasy—*all*, that is, is phantasy. What seems to be affirmation is undercut by the same ambiguity that characterizes the poems previously discussed. Perhaps the poet is saying both things at once—that is, "Either I have perceived correctly that Platonic forms constitute reality and that mankind is merely the inanimate shadow of that reality, or else *all* is phantasy—my perception—everything."

The first line of the poem, "For one throb of the artery," reinforces this second reading by suggesting that whatever certainty the poet enjoyed was as short-lived as a single heartbeat. The "throb of the artery" also suggests movement in time toward death and the condition of the "old grey stone" and "old wind-broken tree." Surely any "consolation" that we find in these five lines must have seemed to Yeats a very feeble one at best.

The volume ends with another short poem, "To Be Carved on a Stone at Thoor Ballylee." The stone, doubtless the same one

20 *Ibid.*, 168.

the poet sat on in the previous poem, is to record only the fact that Yeats, the poet, restored this tower for his wife George, "With old mill boards and sea-green slates":

> And may these characters remain
> When all is ruin once again.

Here Yeats seems for the moment to abandon his faith in a cumulative progress in human affairs as suggested in *A Vision*; here it seems that the shifting motions of the gyres do not alter endlessly, but rather repeat themselves in as self-contained a form as the sands of an hourglass. The future that has absorbed the poet's attention throughout this volume promises, ultimately, to bring all to ruin "once again." Nevertheless, it is important that Yeats's inscription on the rock is as ambiguous in its way as the earlier poems. In one sense, when all is ruin once again, the rock will contain nothing but the record of a failure to restore the tower permanently, like the proud inscription on the statue of Shelley's "Ozymandias," to which this poem invites comparison. In another sense, however, the inscription bears an important historical message, the basic idea of the "Dove or Swan" section of *A Vision*: the cyclic recurrence of historical phases (though the question of *progress* remains moot). The tower was built and destroyed, then rebuilt by Yeats, who wisely anticipates a second destruction—and, no doubt, a second rebuilding, and so on. If he expects all to come to ruin again, he enjoys at least the grim consolation of sharing his insight into the patterns of history with men who are yet to be born. Ozymandias, naively proud, was defeated by the arrogant words that outlived his image and himself; Yeats, wisely humble, triumphs over time. It is a quiet and noble inscription, a fitting conclusion to a noble volume of poetry.

Visionary wisdom, then, in the immutable form of art, is all that Yeats is prepared to pose against mutability as he transposes the germinal doctrines of *A Vision* into poetry. Artistically, at least, it is quite enough.

Index

"Adam's Curse," 88, 94, 95–96, 98
"Aedh Pleads With the Elemental Powers," 36*n*, 41*n*
Aestheticism, 8–20, 25, 34
"All Things Can Tempt Me," 106, 111–12, 113
"Among School Children," 9
"Anashuya and Vijaya," 20, 26, 27–28, 45–46, 48
"Another Song of a Fool," 160
Apuleius: *The Golden Ass*, 33
"Arrow, The," 98
"At Galway Races," 105, 120
"At the Abbey Theatre," 106, 130

"Ballad of Father Gilligan, The," 43–44
"Ballad of Father O'Hart, The" 21, 44
"Ballad of Moll Magee, The," 21, 42
"Ballad of the Foxhunter, The," 21, 29
Baudelaire, Charles, 140
Blake, William: "The Lamb," 19; *Songs of Innocence*, 18; *Songs of Experience*, 18; "The Tyger," 19, 137; *The Marriage of Heaven and Hell*, 140; mentioned, 2
Blavatsky, Helen, 3
"Broken Dreams," 150
"Brown Penny," 113, 114
Burne-Jones, Sir Edward, 70

"Cat and the Moon, The," 160–61
Celtic Twilight, The, 61–62
"Circus Animals' Desertion, The," 32, 40, 68
"Cold Heaven, The," 115, 132–34
Coleridge, Samuel Taylor: "Dejection: An Ode," 68; "Kubla Khan," 132
"Collar-Bone of a Hare, The," 153, 154, 156
"Coming of Wisdom With Time, The," 109–10, 113
CROSSWAYS, 4, 7–29, 31–65 *passim*, 83, 96, 97, 154
"Cuchulain's Fight With the Sea," 43, 48, 49, 50–51

"Dawn, The," 153
"Demon and Beast," 164–66

"Double Vision of Michael Robartes, The," 161–62
"Down by the Salley Gardens," 20, 47
Dublin University Review, 18

"Easter 1916," 131, 158, 163–64
Edward VII, 91
"Ego Dominus Tuus," 156–59, 163
Emmet, Robert, 126
"Ephemera," 20, 21, 23–24, 27, 28, 42
Escapism, 2, 8–25, 53, 66
"Everlasting Voices, The," 75

"Falling of the Leaves, The," 21, 23
Farr, Florence, 124
"Fergus and the Druid," 42, 47–48, 49–55 *passim*, 60, 63, 72
"Fiddler of Dooney, The," 66, 84–85
Fitzgerald, Edward, 125
"Folly of Being Comforted, The," 88, 98

Gonne, Maud, 33, 34, 55, 58, 61, 75, 98, 104, 107, 108, 109, 112, 133, 147–48, 152
GREEN HELMET poems, 87, 103–14, 115, 118
Gregory, Lady Augusta, 106, 124, 126, 127
Gregory, Robert, 153
"Grey Rock, The," 121–24, 126, 129, 131

"Happy Townland, The," 97, 99–103
"Heart of the Woman, The," 82–83
Hegel, Georg Wilhelm Friedrich, 140
"He Bids His Beloved Be at Peace," 80
"He Gives His Beloved Certain Rhymes," 78
"He Hears the Cry of the Sedge," 79–80
"He Mourns for the Change That Has Come Upon Him and His Beloved, and Longs for the End of the World," 70, 77, 84
"He Remembers Forgotten Beauty," 78
"He Tells of a Valley Full of Lovers," 79
"He Tells of the Perfect Beauty," 77
"He Thinks of His Past Greatness When a Part of the Constellations of Heaven," 79
"His Dream," 107
Homer, 73
"Hosting of the Sidhe, The," 72–74, 85
"Hour Before Dawn, The," 130
Hyde-Lees, George (Mrs. William Butler Yeats), 137

Imagery: apocalyptic, 65–86, 90, 92; fire, 77–79; hair, 45–46, 80, 83; mask, 19, 93–96, 104, 110–12, 157; moon, 96–98; rose, 33–36; star, 27–29, 37–38, 46–47, 60, 81; sun, 97–98
"Indian to His Love, The," 20, 21–23, 27, 44, 154
"Indian Upon God, The," 20, 42
IN THE SEVEN WOODS, 87–103, 104, 108
"In the Seven Woods," 89, 90–94, 150
"Irish Airman Foresees His Death, An," 153, 155

Keats, John: *Ode to a Nightingale*, 76–77; mentioned, 157

"Lake Isle of Innisfree, The," 11, 44–45
Lane Hugh: and pictures controversy, 115, 124–25, 136
"Lapis Lazuli," 127
Last Poems, 127
"Leda and the Swan," 60
"Lines Written in Dejection," 157
"Living Beauty, The," 156
"Lover Mourns for the Loss of Love, The," 84

"Lover Tells of the Rose in His Heart, The," 67–68, 70–71, 74

"Madness of King Goll, The," 21, 26, 28, 37, 38, 45
"Magi, The," 115, 132, 134–35
"Maid Quiet," 66, 91–92
"Man Who Dreamed of Faeryland, The," 59, 62
"Mask, The," 104
"Meditation in Time of War, A," 167
"Meditation of the Old Fisherman, The," 20, 21
"Men Improve With the Years," 155
MICHAEL ROBARTES AND THE DANCER, 4, 144, 162–68
"Michael Robartes Asks Forgiveness . . . ," 84*n*
Moore, George: *Ave*, 120
Moore, Sturge, 15
"Mountain Tomb, The," 136
Murphy, William, 117, 126

Nature: Yeats's attitude toward, 8, 25–29, 37–38, 96, 98
Neo-Platonic elements, 40, 66, 89, 138
"Never Give All the Heart," 94–95, 110
"No Second Troy," 113

"O Do Not Love Too Long," 88
"Old Men Admiring Themselves in the Water, The," 94, 95, 98
O'Leary, John, 126
"On Woman," 149–50

Parnell, Charles, 126, 136
"Paudeen," 129
"Peacock, The," 129
"People, The," 152
"Phases of the Moon, The," 146, 159–60, 163
Plato: *Republic*, 33; *Symposium*, 135; mentioned, 33, 167
"Players Ask for a Blessing on the

Psalteries and on Themselves, The," 88, 99
"Poet Pleads with the Elemental Powers, The," 60
"Poet to His Beloved, A," 77
Pollexfen, William, 125
"Prayer for My Daughter, A," 29

"Ragged Wood, The," 96, 97
"Reconciliation," 113
"Red Hanrahan's Song About Ireland," 98
RESPONSIBILITIES, 69, 115–36, 145
Rhymers Club, 121, 122, 123
ROSE, THE, 31–63, 65, 67, 96, 115, 123
"Rose of Battle, The," 32–33, 46, 53, 56–60, 72
"Rose of Peace, The," 53, 54, 55–56
"Rose of the World, The," 53, 54, 56
Rosicrucianism (Order of the Golden Dawn), 3, 34, 70, 138

"Sad Shepherd, The," 18–19, 25, 26, 27, 37
"Sailing to Byzantium," 101, 150, 158
"Saint and the Hunchback, The," 160
Salkeld, Cecil, 138
"Second Coming, The," 163, 165, 166
"Secret Rose, The," 35*n*, 80
Shakespear, Olivia, 7, 75
Shelley, Percy Bysshe: "Ozymandias," 16, 168; "A Defense of Poetry," 116; mentioned, 2, 16, 33, 148
Social attitudes, 105–107, 120–21, 128–29
"Solomon and the Witch," 162–63
"Solomon to Sheba," 155, 156
"Song, A," 156
"Song of the Happy Shepherd, The," 11–19, 26, 27, 37, 44, 49, 52, 93
"Song of the Last Arcadian, The."

See "Song of the Happy Shepherd, The"
"Song of the Old Mother, The," 76, 77–78, 83, 84
"Song of Wandering Aengus, The," 78
Sophocles, 43
"Sorrow of Love, The," 35
"Stolen Child, The," 20
Synge, John Millington: *Playboy of the Western World,* 119; mentioned, 85

Theosophical Society, 3
"These Are the Clouds," 105, 130
"Three Beggars, The," 136
"Three Hermits, The," 127–28, 129
Tir-na'n Og, 2, 20, 73
"To a Friend Whose Work Has Come to Nothing," 126–27, 129
"To an Isle in the Water," 20, 42
"To a Shade," 117, 126, 136
"To a Wealthy Man Who Promised a Second Subscription to the Dublin Municipal Gallery If It Were Proved the People Wanted Pictures," 125, 136
"To a Young Beauty," 156
"To Be Carved on a Stone at Thoor Ballylee," 167–68
"To Ireland in the Coming Times," 49, 63, 123–24
"Tom O'Roughley," 151–52, 153, 164
"To My Sister," 25

Tone, Wolfe, 126
"To Some I Have Talked With by the Fire," 45
"To the Rose Upon the Rood of Time," 33, 36–41, 44, 49, 53
"Travail of Passion, The," 78–79
"Tree of Life, The," 41, 54
"Two Songs of a Fool," 160
"Two Trees, The," 51–52

"Unappeasable Host, The," 83–84
"Under the Moon," 97
"Upon a House Shaken by the Land Agitation," 106

Vacillation, 39–40
"Valley of the Black Pig, The," 34*n*, 78
Vision, A, 1–5 *passim,* 24, 31, 50, 52, 55, 62, 89–109 *passim,* 122, 131–36 *passim,* 137–68.

Wanderings of Oisin, The, 2, 7, 37, 154
"Who Goes With Fergus," 47, 62–63
WILD SWANS AT COOLE, THE, 144, 145–62
"Wild Swans at Coole, The," 145–49
WIND AMONG THE REEDS, THE, 5, 35, 45, 65–86, 87, 90, 96, 109, 115
"Withering of the Boughs, The," 97, 98, 130
Wordsworth, William, 25